The Cry of Our Hearts

Through it all, I was raised by the hand of Jesus

and my heart belongs to Him.

Pat Padgett

Forward

I am Kristi, the daughter of the author, Pat Padgett.. She is, and always has been an inspiration to me and anyone who has had the pleasure of knowing her. She is a wonderful Christian woman and is continually growing in her relationship with God. I am honored to have the opportunity to sit under her ministry.

My Mother is a beautiful, intelligent, multi-talented woman whose life has been an extraordinary journey.
In writing this book she is sharing things that in her past have rendered her vulnerable and left her feeling helpless, but through Christ she was able to rise above and seek comfort that only God can provide.

My family and I encouraged her to tell her story because we felt that it would be a blessing to others and should be shared. We cheered her on throughout the process and continue to support her in any way we can. We lost my Dad in 2016 and it felt like my Mom's grief was insurmountable yet she continued to minister and be a bright light to those around her. We all suffered from his not being with us, it was devastating, but he was the love of my Mom's life and by God's design they were destined to be together so his passing was a much greater loss for her.

In her story She has shared humor, hardship, and happiness, but most importantly she has shared the many ways God provided the protection and guidance that was much needed in her all too tumultuous life. It is her story but is inclusive of her family and friends. While reading you will see the many ways she had to rely on God as so many people in her life have let her down. In sharing her experiences, good and bad, I am sure she is hoping that others will see the realm of possibilities on how to increase their own faith.

My Mother's love of music began at a very early age and has continued throughout her life. She sings, plays the guitar, organ and various other instruments and is self taught on most of them. She has also written many beautiful songs and has shared a few of them in her book. She has blessed many with her singing and playing and has never been hesitant to share her talent.

I am grateful that my Mother took the opportunity to share her story and I am hopeful that it will bless all who read it.

Kristi Trujillo

The Cry of Our Hearts

By Pat Padgett

I guess I should tell you a little about my Mother, before she married my Dad. She came from a poor family who lived on Sand Mountain, in Ider, Alabama. They moved from Sand Mountain to Chattanooga, TN, after Mother and her siblings were grown.

They lived in an upstairs tenement on Broad Street. My mom met my dad there; he lived in a room down the hall. They began to visit in the hallway. They would sit out by the window every night and visit. My dad asked her to marry him, and she said, "yes". It was at this point that my mom began to hear people crying and weeping, uncontrollably, in her mind. It went on for three weeks until the day she married my dad; then it stopped. My mom felt it was the Lord warning her not to marry him. From then on, it was *"the cry of my mother's heart"* … and, also, from us children as we came along.

My dad was from Corinth, Miss., on the border of Tennessee. He came from a family of farmers. They were poor people struggling to make a living. They were a rough bunch. You never heard anything about God in their presence.

I am sure it was a shock to my mom to suddenly be thrust into a family of "roughians". The only one I considered good was my little red-headed Mamaw, my dad's mom. We sure loved her; but the rest we were mostly afraid of.

I came into the world in Chattanooga, TN…a 10-lb baby girl. Daddy was disappointed … no boy! The first whipping I got from my dad was at 6 weeks old. My mother was so afraid I was injured, **but God took care of me**. One thing I must say, before I go any farther… God was always there, taking care of me, and my mother and the other children, all through this long nightmare of life.

My dad was called to the Army, so he gave my mother a talking to, about how to take care of everything. He told her how to take care of Sue and me. He told Mother, if I didn't mind her, to whip me until I peed all over myself… then whip me,

1A

Tommy
Watts
My Dad

Meedell
Watts
My Mother

Pat
Watts
7 years

Pat
Sue
Carol

again, for peeing. Mother had me and Sue to take care of then, and she was pregnant with Carolyn.

We moved in with my Mamaw Holland, my mother's mom; mother's two sisters lived there, too. It was fun to be there with them, after the oppressive way dad made us live.

It wasn't the easiest way to live, but we made it. We were in an upstairs apartment. I slept on the floor, on a pallet, every night. And that is when and where I had my first experience with the Lord. I was only about 4 years old, but I remember every detail like it was today. To set the stage, my mother had taken us to visit her oldest brother and his family in Calhoun, GA. Really, though, my mom had left my dad and was hiding from him. We stayed three weeks. I loved playing with the children who were my cousins. The three I played with were older than I was, so they took care of me.

The night we got back home to Mamaw's I had a dream. My cousins and I were crawling through a dark tunnel. We could see *the bright light at the end of the tunnel*. My cousins were faster than I was, so I was behind. Then suddenly, there was a man with a white robe and longish hair, and a bearded face, in the tunnel with me. He had a huge sword, and he cut my legs off. I woke up screaming. Mother was trying to calm me. Later, after I began to serve God and understand His word, I also began to understand what God was showing me.

He was showing me that my life would be lived for Him. He would direct my path, my way of walking was cut off, and I would walk God's way. I would be brought to my knees many times. But before I could overcome the darkness of my life, God would have to take control and lead me into the light of His word... to the bright *light at the end of the tunnel*.

When I was two years old, I drank gasoline from a soda bottle. I lost my breath because some got in my lungs; my mother packed lard down my throat, and I got over it. The doctor said she saved my life.

My mother would let me go spend the night with my Aunt Dean sometimes. She and my Uncle Brady had a small store and produce stand. I loved being with my Aunt Dean. Back then, they had small boxes of peanuts, and sometimes you would get a box with a dime in it. One evening I got one with a dime in it, too. My aunt and uncle had a relative by marriage named Forrest Townsend… I loved him. But he would scare me and tell me about "Ole Bloody Bones" that lived down the hill behind the store. That night he bought me a box of peanuts and there was a dime in it. He told me old Bloody Bones wants that… you better give it to him. So, I threw them down the hill, the dime and all. Aunt Dean read him the riot act over that one!

I loved staying with Aunt Dean. She was so good to me. She didn't let me get away with anything. She begged my mother to give me to her and Uncle Brady. Of course, mother thought that was unreasonable.

One day my aunt and I were walking down the street. There was a black-headed, freckled-faced boy, older than me, playing on the sidewalk. He threw a rock and it hit me. I cried and he ran. I found out that Barney, the man who became my husband later in life, lived right down the street from my Aunt Dean; and he had black hair and freckles. Could that have been him then?

Another time, my mother got fed up and left my dad, again. He was so mean to her…kept her home like a prisoner. She took me, Sue, and Carol (who was the baby then) and we went to her mom's house. My daddy found us… he was so mad. He slapped my mother, broke her glasses, which cut her eye, and blood was running down on the baby's little gown. Aunt Magalene tried to help, but he just pushed her aside. My Mamaw, my mother's mom, tried to stop him. He picked her up bodily and sat her on a stool. Then he forcefully took us away from our mother. He took us to Georgia, to his brother's place, and paid his niece to babysit us.

I was about 5 years old, I think, when I decided that I was going to try to get Sue and I out of the turmoil. I thought I would take our lives and go to heaven. There was already too much pain and heartache in our small lives. I took Sue and we went down to the orchard. We sat down and I said, "now I lay me down to sleep." I had an old, rusty sling blade, or sickle, that they used to cut cane with. I really don't know what I was going to do. We were both crying. My cousin found us there and I told her what we were doing. She started crying, too. She said, no, that I couldn't do that; that it was wrong. She told me, "Your Mother and Daddy love you too much, even though they get mad."

After my dad got home from the service in the Army, we moved around a lot. My mother had Carol Dean before dad got home, and so he thought the baby wasn't his. He came in on leave, and she got pregnant. My mom was a "fertile Myrtle". Carol looks more like our dad than our mom.

Before my dad finally decided to settle down in Mississippi, we lived all over Tennessee. At one point, we moved to California; we lived in a very high, upstairs apartment, and we were fascinated by the Spanish language there. Later, we moved back to Tennessee and lived in St. Elmo. And after that, we lived in Telehoma, Tenn. And I believe we lived in Oak Ridge, Tenn., for a short time, but I am not sure; then to Tiftonia, Tenn. That is where I started school, in first grade. I remember I had a little girlfriend, Carlene, who was a red head. We lived in a big white house, with green shutters. Mother was pregnant with Tommy then. When she went into labor, it scared me so; I was afraid she would die. Tommy wasn't breach, but he was "folded". He came out buttocks first. Daddy got a little black lady, a midwife, to deliver the baby. She had her little black bag, and I thought the baby came in that little black bag!

Now and then, we had chicken and dumplins. If an old hen started crowing, she went in the stew pot. Mother always said, "a whistlin' woman and a crowin' hen, always comes to some bad end."

I was just 6 years old when Tom Thumb (Tommy) was born, so I took care of Mother…or I thought I did. I would make her soup, cereal, and take her the "thunder bucket" when she needed it. And this set the pattern for my life. Every time Mother had a baby, I was taken out of school to help her. When it was planting time, I was taken out of school; when it was gathering time, I didn't start school with the rest of the kids. I was always behind! I loved going to school, and I loved learning. Sometimes we walked a long way, sometimes we rode a bus. There in Tiftonia, we moved from the big white house to a little brown, two-room house, right down the road.

Daddy was always raising the "ole Billy" stick, sometimes hitting my mom, and beating on me. The neighbors must have heard because one morning, when Daddy started out for the day, there was a large bundle of hickory switches on the porch from the KKK. It really scared my dad. The next day Mother was sorting clothes from a box and there was a large copperhead snake coiled up in it. It was right at the foot of the cot I slept on.

It scared my mother so, she leaped up on the dining table, ran across it, and jumped off. I was sweeping the floor; I was stunned by those antics. The neighbor came over and got it out and killed it. He hung it on the fence, so it would rain!! Daddy came home a few days later, after the switches, and backed his truck up to the porch and came in and told mother we're moving. He said, somebody's been here; there are tracks like high- heeled shoes. Mother said, "my brother came by and brought me a mirror, some pens, and gospel tracks (pamphlets). She reached out the pen to show my dad and her little hand was shaking so.

Daddy asked, "did he have a woman with him?" Mother told him no. He slapped her hard and said, "you're lying!" I was so scared. Mother cried and started packing. He wanted to know where the snake came from. Mother told him what happened; he cussed her out for having a man in our house!

Well, we moved once again to Monteagle Mtn. for a while. And at some point, during this time, we moved to Mississippi. We lived in a log cabin that had a dirt floor. We had an outdoor privy, and no water inside. There was a spring down the hill, but for drinking and cooking, we had to carry water from my aunt's place down the road. Once a week, Mother did laundry on a washboard. And I had to carry water from the spring for that. I hated it because I would see a snake. Sue would go with me and carry a little syrup bucket full of water back. One day she stepped on a snake. I screamed and we ran, and we dropped our water. As Mother would say, we had to "lick our calf over" (get more water!!) One time I was going down the road to my aunt's place to get water, I saw a snake on the side of the road. It looked like it had horns sticking out of its mouth. I hurried back to the house to tell Mother and Daddy. He went down the road and found it. He told us it had a frog in its mouth; the legs were sticking out. They got a laugh out of that.

One day my aunt and uncle came up to visit; that was my dad's sister and brother-in-law. By the way, it was their log cabin, and I do not know if Daddy paid rent or not. Anyway, when they left after the visit, my dad accused my mom of looking at my Uncle Bill too much and started hitting her. She ran from him; I got in the bed and covered up my head. Daddy got mad at my Aunt Dora and Uncle Bill,

Pat w/ TWINS

Alice   Nancy

4A

Pat Sue Carol Tommy

Carol   Don Holland   Sue   Tammy   Leah   Diane Ford   Billy   Danny Shook   Betty   Sheila

Pat was Aunt Dean

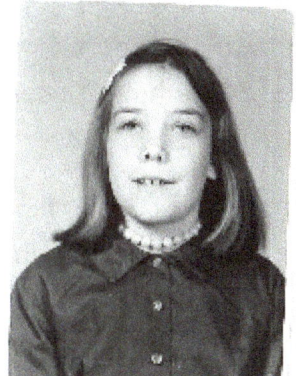

SCHOOL DAYS 1957-58
BELL Carol Watts

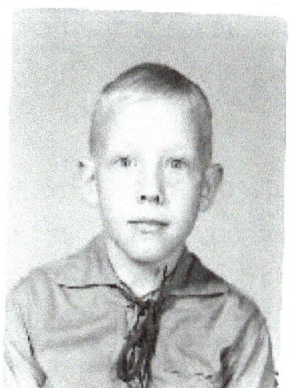

SCHOOL DAYS 1957-58
BELL Leon Watts

so we moved and went to Marked Tree, Arkansas. Mother was pregnant with Leon at the time. We lived on the St. Frances River, back off the highway.

One night, Mother went into labor, but she could not seem to have the baby. Daddy got scared and sent me running to the neighbor's, about a mile down the river. I was running down the riverbank. The farmers had brought men from Mexico to gather the crops. It was November and they were swimming in the cold river water, and some of them were naked...scared me so bad.

I really was doing the 100-yard dash by the time I got to the neighbors. I told them what was happening. They jumped into the truck and took off around the highway; their grown daughter walked me back along the river.

When we got within earshot, we could hear the baby crying. Talk about relief! The baby was an 11-lb baby boy. They named him after our Uncle Raymond, Raymond Leon. So now there were 7 of us: 3 girls, 2 boys, and Mom and Dad. We moved into another house, up the highway, when it became available. We had a huge okra field, and we were surrounded by soybeans. It was about that time that my dad's oldest brother passed away and Daddy went to the funeral. He was really hurt and grieving.

I will back up here. While we were on the river, we had a heavy-duty storm. My dad claimed he did not believe in "all that garbage", meaning God's word. But when that storm was going on, he was asking Mother to pray; our house was shaking so badly. The next morning, the house was moved over on the foundation about 3 inches.

One day, when Mother was bathing Tommy (we called him Chipper), he had a seizure. Mother was so scared; they took him to the doctor, and the doctor told them it was epilepsy. They got a prescription for him as he started having grand mal seizures daily.

There was an Army barracks across the highway where they housed the men that came from Mexico to work the crops. That part of the country was so flat you could see forever and never see the horizon...cotton and soybean fields as far as you can see. My mother did not like Arkansas, and neither did I. I like lots of great oaks and tall, slender pines. Eventually we moved back to Mississippi and Daddy started farming.

While we were still in Chattanooga, before Arkansas and Mississippi, we lived in a little 2-room house on 37th St. My Aunt Dean would come to see us, and she would bring me paper dolls and little scissors, or bubbles, or crayons and a coloring book. As soon as she left, Mother would gather it up and throw it away because Daddy did not want me to have them. I would just cry. I was only about 5 years old. Even though I am an older woman now, I still like bubbles and paper dolls. Sometimes I sit on the porch and blow bubbles. I guess we always want what we cannot have.

At one time, I wanted to be a country western singer, but God had other plans for me. I got to sing for Jesus. "He's the joy of my salvation, yes, He is." I went from a Stella guitar to a Harmony flat top, to a Harmony electric with a Gibson amp. I also had a big Kay guitar. Then my community bought me a Yamaha flat top. Afterwards, Barney bought me a Gibson Electric Red…a pretty guitar, it sounded good, too. Later, my son, Gregg, bought a Gibson flat top for me that I am using all the time. But, these instruments, including my Hammond organ, have been used for Jesus in the ministry.

One day, when I was still very young, a little kitty cat came to the house. I loved it. I could touch it. The weather was hot, and we didn't have a screen door, so we left the door open to get some air and that little cat came in. I was sleeping on the floor on a little pallet, and the cat came to bed with me. Being so little, and awakened out of my sleep, I did not know at first what it was. I started screaming and crying. Daddy jumped up and found the cat. He threw it out the door; it hit a tree and broke its little neck. The next morning, it was laying there dead. I was so upset over that.

After a few months, we moved down the hill into a basement apartment. Daddy got mad at the landlord and went to "fist a cuff" so, of course, we had to move…again. While we were living there, a little girl would come to the fence and invite me to come out and play; and, of course, Daddy said no. One day she brought me a rose. Daddy said I could not have it. I cried, so I got a whipping. It seemed like I had never wanted anything as bad as that rose.

I was climbing one day and fell to the cement floor; I blackened my eye, and it made me sick to my stomach. Mother had some Beeman's chewing gum on a high shelf and I was trying to sneak a piece. That is what happens to little sneaks.

When we moved to Mississippi, my dad would rent a farm and share crop for a year. Then we would move to another farm because Daddy could not get along with the landlords.

My Daddy's sister, Aunt Dora Brassfield, lived in Corinth, Miss. She had a nice farm. She had two sons, and they all worked very hard. My little red-headed Mamaw, and Papaw, lived just down the road, in a little house with no electricity and no inside plumbing. When I was in my teens, Mamaw got electricity in the house, and she bought a refrigerator. One of the sons built her a nice little bedroom. As we were growing up, we loved to go Mamaw's house. Daddy wanted us to sit down and be quiet, and not to be playing and laughing like other normal kids. But Mamaw would take us to the back and hand out biscuits with streaked meat, fried crisp...so good. She would have them stashed in the warming closet on her wood cook stove. And she always had beautiful flowers all over her yard.

My Aunt Dora's husband, Bill, died, so she and her sons ran the farm. When we lived in the log house with the dirt floor, I was six years old. My aunt's oldest boy, who we called Sonny Boy, was about 8 or 9, I guess. We played together sometimes. His little brother, Roy Lee, called him J.T..... his name was Joseph Thomas. My Papaw was Thomas Watts. We used to ask Papaw what his name was, and he would tell us, *Thomas Cornelius Christian by home, Patterson Waterson John Henry Joan.* When he was in a good mood, he was funny. I loved to hear him talk, but he drank most of the time. One day he was sitting by the side of the house, in his big chair, and a snake crawled under his chair. Somehow, he became aware of the snake and started yelling at Mamaw (my dad's mom) to come and kill it. He was crippled and needed crutches to get up and walk. Mamaw went to get a hoe, but the snake crawled away before she could kill it. Papaw's antics were so funny, we had to laugh.

My Aunt Dora's sons grew up... Sonny Boy married and had kids...Roy Lee lived with his mother and helped her run the farm. We found out later that Sonny Boy had a brain tumor. We do not know if this is what caused him to do what he did later, or not. One day he went to his mom's house, called his brother out, and accused him of something. Sonny Boy kept telling Roy Lee to tell his mother what he had done, and Roy Lee kept saying, "I don't know, J. T., what you want me to say?" Sonny Boy shot him right there on the porch and killed him in front of his mother. What a tragedy! That was just one of many in this family.

Besides Aunt Dora losing her youngest, two of my uncles lost their first child. My dad's brother, Claude's, oldest son killed himself. My dad's brother, Raymond's, oldest child was electrocuted working on an air conditioner. My dad's children all lived into adulthood and old age. My Uncle Will Watts' kids all lived long lives. So many young deaths in our family, but it seemed to be that God was never acknowledged in their lives.

After Mamaw got her refrigerator, she would make us iced tea. We never had iced tea before, and we loved it. We looked so forward to going to Mamaw's; we would pile in Daddy's ole rattle trap of a truck and there we would go.

Daddy never wanted us to laugh and play or be rowdy. He made us sit and be quiet. Late in the evening, we would hear Daddy's old truck coming down the road. Mother would say, "here comes your dad." We would scurry around and sit by the wall (there were no living room chairs, only those at the kitchen table), quiet as little mice. We never knew if he would be mad or in a good mood. We would watch his face to see if we could tell. My mama would tell us bible verses to learn. If we learned them, we would get a little prize. She would make little gifts for us out of almost nothing at all. She would tell us about the Lord; we never forgot. If our daddy found out, he would tell her not to tell us that "garbage". So, she would tell us not to say it in front of Daddy. I remember the first bible verse I learned by heart:

Ephesians 4:32...And be ye kind one to another, tender-hearted, forgiving one another. Even as God for Christ's sake hath forgiven you.

For a while, Daddy went to night school. We were so glad then; we were able to play games and laugh and run while he was out.

One day, we moved to a place called Sweat's Place; that was the name of the owner. We started out with 3 or 4 cows... milk cows... so we had milk for the kids, a small Farmall tractor, and a few chickens. We had a nice crop of cotton, nice truck patches (fields) with peas, watermelon, peanuts, and corn... and a big garden. It was a lot of work, but Daddy was doing good. Sometimes we had eggs. That first year was a good one; but, by the end of the second year, Daddy was tired of it. He sold the cows, and he stopped buying food for the chickens...they just did not lay much.

We had a dog named Bozo. He went to the field with Daddy every day. Daddy was plowing, turning the ground. He turned up a snake. He tried to get Bozo to kill the snake, but he only wanted to play with it. It made Daddy mad, so he threw his hammer at Bozo. It hit Bozo in the head and knocked his eye out. Bozo came back to the house. It scared us so bad; we didn't know what had happened. Mother thought the old rooster pecked his eye out; it was hanging on his face. When Daddy came home, Mother told him we had cleaned Bozo up and laid him behind the stove. My dad made a statement that stunned us. He said, "I meant to kill him." My mother cried and so did all of us kids; it really hurt us.

The first time that Mother left Daddy... after we moved to Mississippi and before we moved to Tennessee... it broke my heart; I missed her so much. I was so afraid of Daddy. Mother was all I had to depend on.

When we were still living at Sweat's place, Leon was the baby in diapers. Tommy had 2 or 3 grand mal seizures every day, so we kept him tied in a chair most of the time if daddy was gone. If Tommy were not tied into the chair, he would fall out and bloody his face. When Daddy was home, he would let Tommy play. Before Mother left, it was different. One morning I was in the little closet (most houses we lived in did not have closets); I was sorting clothes to do wash. I saw a little tear in the wallpaper with a small bulge underneath it. I checked it out and found an envelope with $6 in it. I knew what was "coming down the pike"; Mother was planning on leaving. I looked farther and found a pillowcase with some of mother's clothes in it; I was so hurt! *"The cry of my heart..."* One morning, we woke up and got out of bed to an empty house. Daddy had left early for town; Mother left, walking through the woods to the highway; I was ten years old then. I had Sue, Carol, Tommy, and Leon to care for. I tried to do it like mother would. We had no electricity and had an open well and outdoor privy. I built a fire and made some hard biscuits and watery gravy; they were not so good. When Daddy came home, and saw Mother was gone, he was shocked; he cursed a blue streak.

Daddy would continue to go to town every day. He didn't have a job; he just hung out in town. He would come home smelling like perfume and had pink stains on his shirt. Mother said, "He has a woman in town." Mother was never allowed out of the house except to go to Mamaw's sometimes. We had a crop of cotton in. One day the man, Mr. Dildy, came by to talk to Daddy about poisoning the cotton for boll weevils. Daddy wasn't there, so he talked to mother. Daddy drove up about that time, so they discussed it. After Mr. Dildy left, Daddy came in and accused Mother of flirting with him. He started hitting her; he made her face swell up and bruise. It scared us kids; we went into our room and stayed quiet while we cried. Mother was pregnant with Billy Wayne, so I understand, with the way she was treated, why she left... but it still hurt. *"The cry of our hearts..."*

I had a hard time taking care of the kids after she was gone. One day I was trying to light the lamp and burned my hand so bad. I had to wash the clothes in a tub with a washboard; I had lots of diapers. Leon was in diapers and, at times, so was Tommy. When Tommy had a seizure, sometimes he would lose his

10 B
Tommy
&
Leon

Tommy Leon Bobby Carolyn
Sue Tommy Betty Sharkin Allen

Ryan

Cousin
Allen
Johnny

Bobby

Bobby Sarah Lowell and Krissy

Carol Sue Pat

10¢

Carol Pat.

Bonney Pat & Carol

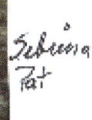

Sebrina
Pat

bowels. The diapers were stained, and I just could not get the stains out. The only detergent I had was Octagon soap. I hung the clothes on the fence, barbed wire at that. Daddy didn't bother to put up a clothesline. When he came home from town, he saw the diapers all stained and beat me badly, and he told me I wouldn't sleep a wink until those diapers were done clean. I started to clean them again, but it was late, and he made me come in and said, "you'll do them tomorrow."

The next morning, after I fed the kids, I started in on the diapers. I'd heard Mother pray, so I started to pray for God to help me get them clean. My knuckles were bleeding, I was scrubbing so hard. Suddenly, someone spoke behind me. I looked around and a little ragged black woman was standing there. She had on shoes with holes in them. She said, "what you doin' little girl?" I told her I was trying to get the stains out of the diapers. She said, "oh, I will tell you how to get the stains out of those "pin hippins". Lay them out on that ragweed. That sort of puzzled me. I looked down at the diapers, wondering how that worked. I looked back at the little lady and she wasn't there. I looked down the driveway; she was nowhere in sight. The Lord had heard me. *"The cry of my heart..."*

I laid those diapers all over the weeds and went in the house to do my chores. Later, I went to see if the diapers were dry, and they were...with no stains! I was so happy. When Daddy saw the diapers, he said, "I knew you could get them clean if you got your head out of your………." What a terrible way to talk to a child. I had worried about the weeds growing so close to the house, because of the snakes... we had copperheads. But right then I thanked God for that ragweed.

One day a dog came to our house. He was a stray... a pretty, white and brown dog. I wanted it to stay with us. But when daddy came home, he tried to run it off. It came right back. Daddy penned it up in the corner of the tractor shed, behind a barrel, and beat it, and cut it up with a shovel. I was devastated; I'd never seen something like that! I cried for that poor dog; it just wanted a home. *"The cry of my heart..."*

When Mother was gone, she had been going to a revival in Chattanooga. There was an Evangelist preacher praying for people. Mother had him pray for Tommy's healing by him laying his hands on her. We couldn't have known about this but, one day, I noticed Tommy's eyes looked different; he wasn't sluggish, and he wanted to play. He wasn't having any spells, as we called them. All day he did not have one spell. Daddy always asked me, "how's the boy, how many spells?" When I told him none, he said, "the (blank) he didn't; you weren't watching him. I ought to stomp you for lying to me." That was just one of his many expletives. But we knew… my brother had been healed by our great God and savior, Jesus Christ. Of course, my dad said, "oh, he just outgrew them."

My mother came home shortly after that… but not before one more incident happened. We were going to Mamaw's on Sunday. I was trying to get all the children dressed but one of Tommy's only pair of socks was lost and I couldn't find it anywhere. Daddy got mad and started hitting me. He knocked me down and my head hit on the bedrail; it knocked me out. When I came to, I was on the bed; Daddy was really scared. When we finally got on the road to Mamaw's, he told me, "don't say nothin'." My head was throbbing, and I was dizzy, but he told me to act normal. I tried. I cried and prayed for mother to come home. **"The cry of my heart…"**

One day we got a letter from Mother; she wanted Daddy to come and get her and bring her home… so he did. We all had a "honeymoon"; things were good for about a month. The only Christmas we ever had was that year during the "honeymoon." Christmas came and we got gifts, but our joy was short-lived. After that, all the hurt and anger with our Daddy started again.

It was then that Daddy went up north to work…hauling cars or something. I am not sure. We enjoyed having Mother at home with us. She told us stories about her trip, about getting prayer for Tommy, and about babysitting…making a little money. She bought me a pretty doll. I named her Barbara. She bought dolls for the other girls, too, and she bought the boys trucks. Then she and Daddy went shopping, the one and only time together. Daddy bought me a teddy bear; it was beautiful. Why couldn't things have always been that way?

Mother was almost due with Billy when Daddy came back from Detroit. He and mother would sit on the front porch and catch up on things; actually, he would grill Mother. I would keep the kids on the back porch. Sue and I would sing; I had learned to do harmony. Daddy heard us and he said, "momma, what's that?" She said, "Oh, it's the girls singing." He sneaked around the house and listened. He was so impressed. He talked to a preacher he knew and got us on his radio show. I remember his name, Brother McCoy. Sue and I sang songs and Tommy said the Lord's Prayer. I was so scared; I had *belshazzer's knees*, one smote against the other. One day we were in the waiting room of the radio station. Daddy had taken us a little early. They were interviewing somebody and, when they finished, he came out… a nice-looking, dark-headed young man … with some other guys. He was friendly to everybody… speaking and nodding, the best I can remember. He patted Tommy on the head... either he or one of his guys. They said he was Elvis Presley. We didn't know who that was, so it made no impression on us... until later. My Mamaw Holland called him "ole Elvis *shaking-all-over* Presley"! It turns out, for some reason, Daddy got mad at the preacher. I think it was because he wouldn't pay Daddy for our singing.

Tommy could say the Lord's prayer. It was so cute, but he couldn't *talk plain*. (That is how we said it in the south.). He had a speech impediment and would say, "Our Fada, who arp in Hebin." When Tommy was a little boy, he really believed in the Lord. And he had an obsession about the wind in the trees. He would spend a lot of time watching the wind blow through them. He would build a little farm and then pretend the storm blew it all away. He would tear it down, knock it around. We asked him sometimes to pray Daddy would bring us bologna for supper; every time he did, Daddy would bring bologna. It was our steak. Tommy has always been a Christian and now he has a gospel radio broadcast, once a week. He has a regular church... his home church... where he and his wife are the music leaders; but he also works in several other churches in Tennessee.

Time is now coming to an end at the Sweat's place. Daddy is working for another farm to share crop. In the meantime, we had a new addition to the family, Billy Wayne; a beautiful little boy was born. Mother's milk didn't agree with Billy, so he cried a lot. They finally got vanilla wafers and pet milk... I would soften the wafers in the milk. I fed him several times a day. He began to do very well. He gained weight and his cheeks pinked up. Mother didn't have much patience with Billy, so I took care of him a lot of the time.

From there, we moved to Murrey's place. It was a new, white, two-bedroom house. It was a pretty place, with lilac bushes and crepe myrtle. There was no plumbing in the house, but there was electricity. For a while, we had lights; we walked around looking at our shadows. Electricity in the house was a novelty.

There were several pecan trees around the house, and I loved pecans. Mother and Daddy wouldn't let me gather any to eat; if they caught me, they threatened to whip me. Sometimes, I would get a chance to pick up a few and sneak to eat them. I never understood why I couldn't have them; they just lay on the ground and rotted.

We went to a school called Gravel Hill. We had to walk but we didn't mind... it was an adventure. There was first through sixth grades in one room, and 7th through 12th in another room... with only two teachers, one in each room.

Daddy wanted to plant 10 acres of cotton. He had a horse called Johnny, and a mule called Big Jim. Daddy worked hard; he turned all the land with Big Jim, getting it ready to plant. He had a little planter to plant the cotton seed, and a fertilizer spreader to distribute the fertilizer. He had to do the fertilizer first, so we used Johnny for that; but Johnny got *skittish* and started jumping around. Daddy got mad, took his knife out and thrust it in Johnny's neck... up to the hilt. Johnny ran away, dragging the fertilizer spreader and, of course, that tore it up and bent the hopper flat. (I never did know what happened to ole Johnny.) Daddy got a pick sack, cut a little bag from it, sewed it up...about 18 inches long by 14 inches around. It came to a point on the bottom with a huge safety pin. That way, he could adjust the flow. He filled it with fertilizer, handed it to me, showed me how to hold it, and the pace to walk so it was not too much or too little. Of course, I got a few knock downs by Daddy before I got the hang of it. We did get the 10 acres of cotton in, plus several patches of peas, beans, peanuts, watermelons, and about two acres of corn. I walked my legs off. I was only 11 years old. Daddy bought some furniture for the house; he even bought drapes for the living room. We had never had curtains on the windows before... just the old-fashioned shades. I remember, when Mamaw and Papaw and my uncle Raymond would come to see us here, they would make homemade ice cream.

It was sometime later that my Uncle Raymond made a deal with Daddy to open a used clothing store over on the highway. Daddy went up north and he hauled a bunch of clothes back to sell but it all fell through. So, he stored the clothes in the old cabin behind our house. He told me I could go get me a couple dresses... I did. I wore one to school, and this girl at the school asked me, "do you wear your mother's clothes?" I was so hurt by that; I thought I looked good. Ha!

There was a huge tractor by the barn. It had metal wheels with cleats on it. We had had a lot of rain, so the wheel was sinking into the mud, and rusting. Daddy wanted to lift the wheels from the mud and set them on boards. While he lifted, I tried to push the board, but I couldn't get the board under the wheels. We tried once again but we couldn't do it. He said I wasn't trying, and he started hitting me. Every time we tried, and failed, he would hit me more. Mother saw him and ran out to stop him. But he ran her back into the house. Finally, I couldn't feel the pain...just the "thump, thump" of my head; I almost passed out. My face was so swollen I couldn't see out of my eyes; they were closed shut. He told me to get in the house. Mother came out to get me and helped me into the house. She was cooking supper, and the baby, Billy, was crying, so she sat me down and put him in my arms. I could barely see the baby's little fuzzy head. I tried to take comfort from his body close to my chest. When I heard the door open and heard Daddy's footsteps, I was so scared. I heard him say to Mother, "did I do that to her?" *"The cry of my heart..."*

At one time, I had a dog named Rusty. I loved him so much. Once Daddy beat him until the dog passed out. I thought he was dead. Daddy threw him over into the woods. About a week later, he came crawling out of the woods to me. He was crippled. About that time, we moved to the Griffin place. I never saw Rusty again. *"The cry of my heart..."*

Mother left Daddy again before we moved from Murray's. She had sent us kids to the field to pick peas that day. Besides myself, I had Sue, Carol, Tommy, Leon, and Billy. She made me take the baby; I wondered about that but, at that time, I didn't suspect anything. When we had picked the rest of the peas, we came home, and Mother was gone. I started to cry and called Mother to please come back. Later, she told me she heard me calling for her but that she had to go. My sister, Sue, made fun of me; she said I sounded like a hound dog howling. But I was so hurt, I couldn't stop. Of course, Daddy was upset but he had me to take care of the kids, so he went on his merry way. Daddy didn't really know what we needed. I needed shoes and he ordered me old woman shoes. I hated those shoes! I had long hair; it had never been cut. It just hung in my face. Whenever I had to build fires to cook, it was a miracle that my hair didn't catch on fire. *God took care of us.* One time Sue threw a butcher knife at me. It whipped right by my head. *God took care of me.* *"The cry of my heart..."*

We had raised sweet potatoes and peanuts; that was about all we had to eat that winter. I've never been so tired of sweet potatoes and peanuts. We would pull those peanuts and lay them on a tarp in the sun. They were very good if you didn't have a constant diet of them.

At one point, before Mother left, Daddy got a wild hair and bought a load of ceramic lamp bases, vases, and bowls, and rented a cinder block building on the highway. He put Sue and I in there to sell those ceramics. We liked it for a while. We sold a few pieces a day. Some of the lamp bases were very pretty. Customers were few and far between; Sue and I stayed all day, and when there were no customers, we would sing. In the evening, daddy would come and pick us up. But when Mother left, I had to stay home all day to take care of the kids.

We never stayed long at any one place. Daddy loved to move on, so we moved to the Griffin place and stayed there a very short time. I guess it was kind of an adventure for the kids, but for Mother and me it was a big job. We didn't stay there very long before we moved to Grant's place. Such a pretty place with all its fruit trees, purple plums, sand plums, lilacs, buttercups…pretty, pretty place.

You know, helping to take care of all those brothers and sisters made me feel like they were part mine. I have so many memories of when all the kids were born and of their childhoods. I cannot really remember Sue as a baby very well, but Carolyn? I held her and helped to take care of her. Mother taught me how to put her in a diaper. We had a baby bed for her. She was wearing shoes that were too big for her. They were high-tops and they turned up at the toes. We called them witch's shoes. Carolyn tried to say it and it would come out "bitch's" shoes. We laughed. She would just say things we would laugh at. She would say, "gobby men" and "I shabby". I don't know where she heard those things, but it was so cute. My memories of my brother Leon were that he was the little man of the bunch. He wanted to help everybody and keep peace; he was a helper.

As young kids, Sue, Carolyn, and I worked in the fields every day, raising the crops. Sue was treated a little better than Carolyn and I were. Mother and Daddy seemed to care more for her. They didn't whip her very much. Mother was hard on Carol; I don't think she was fair with her. So, I would take up for Carol and would get myself some whippings over that. When Tommy got old enough, he went to the field. He was a little stinker, always creating havoc. Leon was my little man. Even though he was little, he would try to help by carrying in the wood for me to cook with. He would try to sweep the floors, but he was so small. Sue was lazy but she was funny and would make us laugh. She pretended she was a chicken; we would find her in the chicken house, on the roost. Carolyn was a slender, always neat, little girl. She was sad a lot, too. I tried to be there for her. She was helpful, like Leon. She had it hard after I left home. Mother would blame her for Sue's misdeeds. It was amazing… all those kids with all those different personalities!

There were good times with Mother, too. She would make us things to play with. It always became a treasure to me. How sweet it was; it brings me to tears thinking about it. It hurt me so badly to see Daddy beat on Mother. Mother would sing and play for us; I loved it when she would sing gospel, pop, and country.

When Leon was little, I carried him around on my hip until he was three years old. He would give me love taps on my cheek, then he would pinch my cheek hard. I would smack him and tell him, "that hurt." He would say, "oooh" and give me another love tap. I loved him like he was my own son.

Billy Wayne was the son born after Leon. He was a beautiful little boy who smiled all the time; he had rosy cheeks, bright blue eyes, and blond, curly hair. Sheila was the 4th girl, born after Billy, at Grants place; she was a breach baby. Mother had a hard time with her. She was a good little baby as she did not cry a lot. Because she was breach, she had a little trouble getting started; she had a slight heart murmur. She was a cute, little, blue-eyed blond. Then Bobby came along. He was just a toddler when I left home. I cried after him, I hated to leave him behind. When the twins, Alice Faye and Nancy Kay, came along, I was living in Chattanooga, so I wasn't with them right away. Mother had them at home. She got up one night to go to the bathroom and Nancy fell out to the floor! Mother called Daddy; he put Mother, and the baby, back in bed. Daddy had almost stepped on the baby because it was so dark. My poor mother realized another baby was on the way. She had been in labor for a couple of hours before Alice came along.

The best I can remember, we moved from Grant's place to Prater's place. It was an old house. There was a large living room, with a fireplace; a long kitchen that ran along the back of the house; and two little bedrooms. There were huge oak trees all around. We thought it was a haunted house. You could hear somebody walking in the kitchen every night. It scared us kids at first, but we got used to it.

Daddy liked to hear Sue and I sing. Tommy and Carolyn sang some, too. So, he went out and bought a black and white Gibson guitar and told mother to teach me to play. My mother was reluctant to teach me to play the guitar. At the time I didn't understand but my dad and she was having an argument. He was cussing my mom because she didn't want to teach me. She only knew 3 chords, but she finally gave in and showed me the chords. She was so curt and short with me. But, as I got older, I understood she was so jealous of me and everything I accomplished. She would criticize me. She said, "I thought I was the only one that could do anything." I was afraid of my Daddy and I wondered why my mother didn't love me. I'm sure she did, but she didn't show me. I tried to understand; she had all the other children to be concerned about. Now I have to give credit where credit is due; my Daddy started me on the guitar, and my mother taught me what she knew. It's been a joy for me all of my life.

Mother left again so I took care of the kids. They were getting bigger. Tommy and Sue were a couple of brats. I couldn't do anything with them. Sue was so lazy; she wouldn't help me. Tommy threw rocks in the window at me while I was cooking them a meal. I'd go after him and he would run up a tree. One day Leon threatened to beat Tommy up if he did it again, and so he stopped. Another day,

Leon was outside playing, and he said I was there. But when he came in, I was at the stove cooking. It scared him so. I didn't quite understand. I knew I couldn't be in two places at one time.

In the evenings, we would sit out under the trees and sing and play the guitar. One evening, with Daddy at night school, and Mother gone, it was just me and the kids. A car came by, full of teenagers. They drove by, then backed up and pulled in. They needed water for their car; it was running hot. I told them to go ahead and draw water; they did and took a drink and filled their radiator. They asked us to sing and so we did. They sat on the ground and listened; a couple of the girls cried. Shortly after, they had to go so they thanked us and drove on down the road.

The old landlord found out Daddy was gone, too, so he would come up to, supposedly, see about us. I was afraid of him. One day he put his hand up Sue's dress; she ran like the wind. I told him I was going to tell Daddy when he came home. The landlord quit coming.

We got to go to Mamaw's quite often while Mother was gone. She would cook a big dinner from her garden…soooo good. She would pull fresh corn; she called them rosners; we called them roasting ears. I loved the way she talked. She would tell us at night to "make haste and lie down"; she would say, "fer me don't feel good."

Mamaw and Papaw had an outdoor privy. There was a time when Papaw was using it; the wind blew it over and Papaw was yelling. We couldn't help but laugh! We had some good laughs with Mamaw and Papaw. One time, when Mamaw was young and raising her kids, she was on the porch breaking green beans. A black snake fell from the rafters onto her lap. Beans went everywhere and Mamaw did a little dance, whooping and hollering!

After Grants place, we moved to Praters, and at some point, we moved back to Chattanooga and lived on Calhoun Ave. Mother had come home at Praters and then left again, so we were alone. I was about 12 years of age, I think. We were going to school. My teacher was Mrs. Grey. She was so good to me. When Mother left, Daddy took me out of school to take care of the little ones. Mrs. Grey came by to see about me. She told Daddy, "I'll come by after school and help her with her lessons." He said, ok, and so she did. I just loved her for that. The next-door neighbor offered to take us to church, and Daddy let us go. One Sunday, the music was beautiful, and the spirit of God was moving. I went to the alter and accepted the Lord into my life. I felt so good and free. Praise the Lord!

When Mother came back again, we moved back to Mississippi. We lived at a place called Billingsley. I am not sure when, but my time of childhood was over. I cramped a lot and I hated it.

We moved to Arkansas again to pick strawberries. It was a hard job we had. Mother had left again, so it was just us kids and Daddy. We lived in a 3-room house in the middle of a cane field; big stalks were sticking out of the ground where they had cut the cane stalks down. We worked all week, and on the weekend, Daddy would stay gone. We had an old pump outside that you had to prime to get water. I used all the prime water, and it wouldn't prime. We were without water all weekend until Daddy came home. We were a thirsty bunch! Needless to say, I got a beaten for that, too. After that, I would pray that I would get water… and it always came. **God took care of it.** We were so glad to leave that hot cane field; we moved back to Mississippi.

We also lived in Hornsby, TN. We lived in a session house (a railroad company house) right by the railroad. The trains coming down the track shook the whole house. I walked to school every day. I loved that school and the kids. My uncle had brought a load of shoes. I invited some of the kids to come pick out a pair of shoes; we had all sizes… so the kids did. And, of course, because of my generosity, I got in trouble.

We didn't live there long. It was called Lambert's place. (I will insert this, fast forwarding to the future: My brother, Leon, became an electrical contractor in Datil, NM, where the Lord sent us. In Datil, he was doing work for a man named Lambert, in Quemado, and found out he was a relative of the man in Hornsby, TN. Small world…)

The best I can remember, we had moved to McCool, Miss., from Arkansas, way out in the backwoods. There might be a car go by once or twice a week. It was one of the most miserable times of my life. I tried to leave there one night. I had me a flashlight and a jacket. But I looked at those little kids and I couldn't leave them, too. Mother was already gone, and Daddy was saying he wasn't going to let her come home again. I was so hurt without my mom. *"The cry of my heart…"* I felt like Mother was all I had. The next day Daddy found out I was wanting to leave. He always did find out these things, so I certainly got a beating.

Shortly after that, Mother came back home. I was so pale, skinny, and a nervous wreck. Mother got really concerned; she didn't like what was happening to me. She made arrangements for me to go to Chattanooga, TN. My mother was concerned because she thought that my dad's actions were inappropriate toward me. And my mother was right... so she put my dad in jail and got me out of town. Two old ladies, who were our neighbors many miles down the road, took me to the bus station. I went to my Aunt Dean's. She gladly took me in, but I had to get a job and pay board to her. I never had a free way to go. I always had to pay. I felt that I was Mother and Daddy's unpaid servant. I was an unsocialized, uneducated, little country girl. But I had to go out into the workplace and make my own way. I didn't feel that my Uncle Brady really wanted me there, but he went along with my Aunt Dean. I had to sleep on a roll away bed, in the bedroom with my Mamaw and my cousin, Donald. Donald was about 7 or 8 years old, and he was the apple of my Mamaw's eye. She resented me being there; I sure felt in the way. The few clothes I had I kept in a cardboard box. But I still felt like I was in heaven compared to being home and used and abused, with nothing to look forward to. I was fascinated by the neon lights along the boulevard's flashing figures. My eyes were huge with wonder. I loved going to church with Aunt Dean and my uncle, but I would beg her to not introduce me to anyone. I was too shy and backward to interact with anyone. I never talked to anyone. I stayed to myself for a long time. I did not feel that I was good enough.

I missed my little brothers and sisters, and my mom, a lot. As soon as I got a job making $15 a week, my mother wrote me a letter asking me for $10 of my $15 each week. When I refused, she wrote and threatened to make me come home. My aunt got so upset; she cried and pleaded with me to send mother the money. I gave in, of course. My aunt always gave in to my mother. My mother knew she could use Aunt Dean; she was an easy touch.

When I first arrived in Chattanooga, I had about 3 days to get acclimated and then started looking for a job. I got a job at the Dairy Gold drive in. I worked one week, and they paid me $6...and I quit. I started looking again and found an ad in the paper.

A man was selling waterless cookware. He needed an assistant to help put on cooking parties at homes. I went out with him several times for a few weeks. The food was good, but I felt so uncomfortable with him. Sometimes he would really be looking at me. I was a pretty girl, but I wasn't really aware of it then. One thing I will say, he was a gentleman to me. Then I heard about a job at Omar's Sandwich

Shop on Chickamauga Ave. in Rossville, GA, a suburb of Chattanooga. They hired me right away. I was a curb hop, taking trays out to the cars, and having to put up with smart aleck boys and their rude remarks. But I did make good tips!

While I was working at Omar's, I met a boy who came to the church I went to. We became engaged; his name was Mickey. His family was not easy to get along with. They were high strung people. They played music and sang really well. But I finally broke off the engagement and, later on, I got engaged to an older guy by the name of Ernest Ewing Courtney. He was very good to me and gave me lots of gifts, but I found out he drank, and I couldn't take that, so I quit him, too.

I met a girl named Betty, at church, and we became friends. She was old enough to be my mother, but she was so good to me and I was very needy. I needed a "mother figure", and she was that for me. She took me on trips and bought me gifts. She took me to work and picked me up. I didn't have to walk to, or go on, the bus then. I got to do and see things I never had before. But, to my sorrow, I found out she was a lesbian. I didn't know what a lesbian was then but found out she was trying to groom me to become her partner. She went to church with us, so I just thought she was a Christian and a good woman. My heart was broken over that. *"The cry of my heart…"*

My Aunt Dean had a cousin from Dallas, TX… Aunt Bea… who would come every summer and stay a month with Aunt Dean. She was a little "woman of the world." She had been a "rounder", but she had become a Christian. I was getting ready for work one morning when Betty came by to visit and take me to work. I wasn't quite ready and came into the dining room in my slip to say hello. Then I hurried on to finish getting ready. After we left, Aunt Bea told Aunt Dean, "you better get that pretty girl away from that old gal. She is a lesbian". My Aunt Dean said, "No, she is a Christian!" Bea asked her, "didn't you see the way she looked at her?" Aunt Dean said no, but she told me about it, and I got plenty mad; I didn't believe it. Then I began noticing how she got mad every time I had a date. I bluntly told her what I had heard and not to come around anymore. She threatened us.

I need to tell this little story before I close out the saga of Betty. She was selling Stanhome products. We had Stanley parties; I helped to set up, decorate, fix snacks, and fill out orders. We had a party, took orders, ate, and fellow-shipped. Somebody suggested we have prayer before we go so everyone turned in their prayer requests. We all knelt at our chairs and prayed out loud… except me; I was too shy. I sat by myself, hoping no one would talk to me.

When we got up from our kneeling positions, I saw a woman across the room, and she was looking at me intently. I turned my head quickly, but I felt her coming my way. I was scared. She said, *"little sister, God has his hand on you. He wants to give you a word. You are called, you have a music ministry and a ministry of the word. God is preparing a man for you, and at the appointed time, I will bring him unto you. You will Evangelize across the country, ministering for me."* I said, OK! That was all new to me. It was 1957; I was 16 and a half years old. Of course, as the months and years passed, I forgot about that word from God.

After I quit running around with Betty, she stalked me. I would see her in her car, at the bus stop, at my work. She would call and hang up, over and over. I am so thankful nothing happened to me. *God moved in time!!* A year later I saw her, with her partner. They were so "butch"... Little Aunt Bea was right.

I dated lots of guys, but I didn't want to get married, and these guys just did not "ring my bell." I was working at the Homeplate Cafeteria, behind the line; I was the pie cutter. The cashier there took a liking to me. She and her family took me on vacation with them to Florida. We had a good time. Their daughter, Sandra, and I picked us up a couple boyfriends to see things with and swim and ride with. It was so much fun. They, Grace and her husband, bought me a pretty bathing suit and bath towel. While I was gone, though, my Mamaw Holland passed away. It was a sad time.

One day on the job, Grace called me to the phone. It was my mother. She said, "Patsy, this is your mother. I've left your daddy for the last time. You'll have to get me an apartment and take care of me." She had Sue and the twins with her. My feathers fell. I felt like I was in prison again. But I did get an apartment for us. I had to buy a ton of coal as we had what was called a monkey heater. It was late Fall, and they had no coats. We had no blankets, or bed clothes; we needed dishes, pots and pans, and silverware. So... I opened accounts and went in debt to furnish the apartment.

After the phone call at work, I went home that evening with a heavy heart. I wanted to see mother and the girls, but I knew it was going to be hard. Sue was a teenager and a smart mouth. I had a hard time with her.

I opened another charge account at a dry goods store for all the domestics. Christmas was just around the corner and I wanted them to have a Christmas. I bought two little, red rocking chairs and two dolls for the babies. I bought Sue a birthstone ring from Zale's Jewelers. I bought Mother an iron and a watch.

Shortly after Christmas, I got a call on the job. Mother was in the hospital; she had had a miscarriage. I didn't even know she was pregnant. I made arrangements to pay, monthly, for the bill. Mother recuperated and got back on her feet. My mother never had a job.

I went to the grocery store close by and asked if I could open an account for groceries and make monthly payments. I knew that they knew the situation; my aunt knew them personally, so I am sure she told them about it. They agreed, and I got groceries every week and paid payments each month.

In the meantime, there was a little snack store next door to where we lived; they sold sodas, chips, ice cream, and candy, etc. Once I was coming home from work and the owner of the store met me outside. He asked if I was going to pay the bill anytime soon. He was also the man I paid my apartment rent to. I asked him, "what bill?" I knew my rent was paid up. He said, "the bill in the store." I said, "I didn't make a bill!" He said, "your mother and sister did." I told him, "I didn't sign, I won't pay." The old gentleman was Mr. Tarply, Betty's dad; I had always liked him. I told him, "you shouldn't have let them sign my name." Needless to say, I told Mother and Sue how the "cow ate the cabbage!" They were mad at me for a while, but they got over it.

I heard they had openings at the Davenport Hosiery Mill. I went and applied; they called me the next day. I went to work for them the Monday of the next week. It was a totally new experience; a shock it was to my tender ears. Those girls were rough and ready. I made more money. I worked third shift, though, so I didn't get enough sleep. Aunt Dean lent me the rollaway bed I had slept on at her house. It was very uncomfortable, and it sagged in the middle. Sue got a babysitting job; that helped a little; that is, when she brought her earnings home. Sometimes she spent it before she got home!

I made some friends at work. I hung out with them quite a bit, but they drank and smoked. On New Year's, we all went out. One of the girls was rich; her dad gave her a new car and a fur coat...fur and suede... for Christmas. She wanted to know if I wanted something to drink. I said, "yes". She said, "what about an orange juice?" I said, "yes." It was good; I think I had about 3 of them...then I was drunk. I was in the back seat with the pretty coat, and I threw up all over it. I heard my friend say to her, "good for you; you shouldn't have done that to her."

That was the only time I got drunk. It made me so sick, I couldn't understand why people like it. I slept for three days.

I had a girlfriend at the hosiery mill who kept after me to go out with her boyfriend's friend. I said no; I was tired of dating. One night, I was home painting the living room walls. My hair was up in rollers, no makeup on, wearing a man's shirt and rolled up jeans. There came a knock on the door. I opened it and there stood a tall, good looking, dark-eyed, dark-haired man. I asked him, "can I help you?" He said, "are you Pat Watts?" and I said yes. He started grinning and told me, "Wanda is in the car and I'm Barney Padgett." My response was, "I'll kill her!" He took off to the car with a big grin on his face. Wanda came in and I jumped her. She said, "just a burger at Mike's, then we'll bring you right back." I said OK. She started fixing my hair and I put on makeup and got dressed, and we took off. I got in the back seat with Barney. He started talking to me. I don't remember what he said, I was so nervous. Wanda and Gary stayed inside Mike's and got us all burgers; Barney and I were alone in the car. He told me all about his business. He was working for Stark Brothers Nursery Landscaping. Later, he drove me around and showed me places he had landscaped. They were beautiful. We started dating regularly. I knew I loved him, but I didn't know if I was *IN* love yet! He asked me to marry him, and it scared me off. I didn't want to marry after what I'd seen between Mother and Daddy. I didn't want any of that. I was so in debt I couldn't see my way out, and I didn't want to bring that into a marriage. During that time, I didn't go to church very much. My Aunt Dean and Uncle Brady would come by and take Mother and the girls to church.

When Barney came to pick me up on the first date, he was driving the pretty convertible that he drove when Wanda came to my house. I said, "why are you driving Gary's car?" He grinned and said, "it's my car; he was just driving for me." I was glad of that. We would go have a burger on our dates. He never took me out to dinner; we just rode around a lot.

Barney asked again to marry me. I said, NO. That week we had plans to go out. But my girlfriend at work, Mercidath, asked me to go home with her up in the country and think things out...so I did. She even had a boyfriend there for me. He was sweet but not my type. They all played music and sang; I enjoyed that. I missed Barney so much. Mercidath came upstairs and found me staring out the window. She said, "you're missing Barney, aren't you?" I said, "yes, I'm sorry." Her family was so sweet to me. I liked her brother, but I didn't realize at the time, God was working in my life and Barney was the man God had prepared for me. Of course, you couldn't tell it at the time. Barney was insufferable sometimes, and I am sure I was, too. Believe me, God knows what he is doing, and he knows just how to bring us around to His way of thinking, but that would be awhile.

When I got back home, Mother told me that Barney came by to pick me up and she told him what I had done. Mother told me I should apologize to him. I felt bad but I let 3 weeks rock on, and I didn't hear from Barney. I finally went and called him. His mother answered the phone. I asked for Barney. She asked me if I was the girl Barney was dating. I told her yes. She said, "well, he's at the doctor; he had an accident." I started crying and she told me that he would be ok. "It's his neck and back; and his knee is messed up. It totaled his car." When Barney got home, she told him, "that girl you're going with is so upset about you." Right away, Barney asked his Pop if he could borrow his car. Pop threw him the keys and Barney came right over. I was so glad to see him.

We went out for a burger and talked. He came back that evening and picked me up again; we went out to dinner and had burgers again. When he drove me home, we were sitting out front in the car. He pulled out the velvet box and asked me to marry him again. The engagement ring was beautiful. I was still reluctant, but I had to say yes.

I was on my own to plan a little wedding; no one to help me; not any money to spend. So, of course, I went in debt for a pretty, white, cocktail-length dress and I had a homemade veil. I already had a nice dress to wear for the honeymoon, and a beautiful orchid corsage.

Back to the honeymoon. What honeymoon?! We were on our way to Nashville when we came upon a roadblock where they were checking licenses and registrations. It was a long line. As we were waiting, Barney wasn't paying attention to the outside of the car, and he started rolling. He hit the car in front of us... just a tap... but the police officer stuck his head in the window and said, "sir, this is what we're trying to avoid." Barney said, "I just got married!!" The officer looked over at me, saw my big corsage, laughed and said, "get on down to Alabama." Barney and I were so relieved and drove on. In a few minutes, it dawned onto us that he said "Alabama". We were on the wrong road! We were able to get back on the correct road and drove awhile. Barney asked if I wanted to stop now; I said yes. We found a Holiday Inn and spent the night. The next morning, we ate breakfast before getting back on the road. Barney asked me, "do you want to go on to Nashville?" Since I had already been to Nashville, I said, "no, let's go home and start our marriage" and so, we did.

My 26A
Mother
one
and
I

Barry 8 year

Barns in Service

Ramey Pinkwell Preacher

I was working at Davenport; of course, Barney did not have a job because of his accident. We were living at Barney's mother's home. (*Side note: Barney had already served in the Air Force... being stationed at Bolivia, Germany, Italy, and France, and some time in Africa...came home and went to college on the GI Bill and taught high school... all before I met him. My family thought Barney was so good looking. I think my mom and sisters all had a crush on him.*)

The girls at Homeplate Cafeteria gave me a bridal shower and gave me some beautiful gifts. A couple of my friends at Davenport gave me gifts, but I did not have a home shower. Barney's mother gave me a beautiful bedspread, and a large cook pot that I still have. My Aunt Dean and Uncle Brady were at our wedding, and Uncle Brady and Mother said they felt the Holy Spirit in a special way. **God was moving...**

While we were still living at Mom's, I had a miscarriage because of my appendix. It was so inflamed that it almost burst. I was out of work for a few days, but Barney had gone back to work, so I did not go back to my job.

While we lived at Mom's, I became real good friends with Pop. I really loved him like a dad. He was a good Christian man. Mom was working every day. On Friday, when her work week was over, we would get in the car and go to this good BBQ place up on the highway and have dinner. Barney was working late so he ate with his boss. That way, it was Mom, Pop and I; I felt so included.

I helped Mom paint her apartments; she had rental properties. We painted the walls, the ceilings, and the porches. One day, Mom decided we would paint Pop's old car. We painted it with brushes, inside and out. Even though it had some brush strokes in the paint when we were done, we had fun doing it and it looked nice and clean. Mom also taught me to sew. We made matching dresses for her and me.

Barney and I moved into an apartment owned by Mom and Pop. It was a big house; our apartment was three large rooms and a bath, and an enclosed back porch. Mom and I decorated it. I was pregnant with Gregg while we lived there. I was also getting my teeth pulled. They started to crumble when I got pregnant. Then I had the old-fashioned measles for three weeks; I was so sick. The family did not tell me, but they were afraid Gregg would be damaged because of the measles.

About this time, my sisters Carolyn and Sheila left home. They just decided to run away one day. They were walking down the 72 Highway in Corinth, Miss....it

was raining. A woman was on her way home when she saw them and stopped. She asked them, "where are you going?" They told her, "to our mother." She said, "where is your mother?" And they told her she was in Chattanooga, Tenn. She told them to get into her car and she would see what she could do.

This woman, who was the Sheriff's wife, took them home with her and called her husband. She fed them and gave them a bath; that is when she saw the dark bruises on both girls. They told her that their daddy did it. The wife explained to her husband about them wanting to go to their mother. He mentioned that he had some friends going to Chattanooga the next day and would see if they would take the girls to their mother. They said they would be glad to and would take them directly to her. That sheriff knew my dad and he had heard the talk. So, again, *God moved for the children*. Mother had a big surprise when they showed up at the door. The man asked, "are you Maebell Watts?" When she said yes, he said, "I've got two little girls for you." **God moved again**. Mother had moved into her own apartment, and she had gotten a divorce from daddy. She was a Christian woman and went to church every week. She was also now dating again.

Barney and I decided then to move to Miami, Florida. We got an apartment for a couple of months and then bought a three-bedroom house. I was so happy for a home of my own. I decorated it and landscaped my yard, and I built a rock garden with lots of pretty flowers and plants. Barney bought a shower door/tub enclosure business, including a truck, from his brother-in-law. He installed the tubs and shower enclosures in fancy hotels on Miami Beach.

I was totally ready to have a baby. Our Gregg was a beautiful 9 lb., 4.5 oz. baby boy. Barney and his sister painted the nursery a pretty baby blue while I was in the hospital. Sue and I had gone to the thrift shops and the Goodwills and bought real good furniture for the baby's room. By the way, my baby was healthy, my family worried for naught.

Things rocked on but Barney and I weren't getting along very well. I had a talk with Barney and told him I could not raise my child in the midst of fighting and fussing. I told him that was how I was raised, and it made me a nervous wreck. I wanted a Christian home. Barney surprised me by asking, "so where do you want to go to church?" I told him, "wherever you want to go." He suggested we try the First Baptist church on Bird Road... I said yes. The pastor and deacon came over and prayed and talked with us.

We quickly became a part of the church. Barney and I were both in the choir, and Barney became an usher. We went every Sunday. But, more importantly, our lives changed. We gave our hearts and lives to God and it became a happy life. Every Sunday, when we got home from church, I would start preparing lunch and Barney would say, "I think I'll go pray till you get dinner ready."

I had a spare bedroom with just a bed …but it was made up of only a mattress and box springs set on four concrete blocks. I noticed, when I went to straighten the bed, that it would almost be off the blocks. I wondered about that. I finally asked Barney what was happening in there. He said, "well, babe, I don't really understand but the spirit comes over me so strongly, it shakes me all over." I told him God was doing something for him…but I didn't understand it either.

Barney said to me later, "I don't think we're getting what we need in this church." (Now I must interject here. When Barney and I first got married, I took him to my mother's church, a Pentacostal. Maybe you don't know how they worship, but they are loud, are shouting, speaking in tongues, and dancing in the spirit. When we left after church was over, walking to the car, Barney said, "Man these people are strange; I am not going back there!"

(Back to current…) I asked Barney, "where can we go to church?" He said, "well, maybe we can go to a church like your mother goes to." My knees almost buckled, but I was willing. I got the phone book and looked for a church; I chose a Church of God.

We started the next Sunday and we loved it. The people embraced and received us well. They had beautiful music and singing, and the preacher was really anointed. I never had felt the spirit as powerful as that. I had never reacted to the moving of the spirit except to cry and pray to myself. But one Sunday, while the preacher was preaching, I just stood to my feet, with my hands in the air; I felt like I was going to fly away. God was moving in our lives; little did we know what was going to happen.

Barney's sister, Sue, was watching us as our lives changed, and she saw the change. She told me one day, "I believe you and Barney are doing the right thing. That was really something for her to say because she didn't believe in anything spiritual. We loved going to that church and we were growing in the spirit.

One day, Barney came home and said, "I feel like God wants us to go back to Chattanooga. We had bought a 3-bedroom home with a big yard that I had landscaped and built a pretty rock garden in, and there was a large screened-in sun porch. I had fun with flowers out there; Gregg loved it and he would roll his walker around in there. He would spring up and down in his jumper chair. And I had an exercise machine there, too.

We put our home on the market and it sold right away. We hired an Atlas moving van and took our furniture to Chattanooga. We rented a house after we got there, and we moved in right away. I wasn't feeling very well; I went to the doctor and he told me I was pregnant but that I had low blood sugar… I was anemic. He gave me five different meds and I was throwing up all day. I was one sick gal.

Again, God moved for me. There was an evangelist in town…the one that had prayed for Tommy when he was healed of the epilepsy. I went that evening with Barney. The evangelist picked me right out of the crowd and prayed for me. I was healed; I never had to take that foul-tasting medicine again. I got fat and so healthy after that and I had healthy 9 lb., 11.5 oz. baby girl, Kristi Michele. Around the same time, Barney's stepdad had a double hernia. He went to the revival meeting and was completely healed. That little preacher told him, "you can take that truss off now; you are healed."

We had moved to a duplex on Duncan Ave. I was so happy; I felt my family was complete. Although, after Kristi was born, we were having a hard life. Barney wasn't working. Mom and Pop would bring us groceries. One day, they came over and invited me to go shopping with them. I thought we were going to a grocery store, but we went to a furniture store instead. They showed me a rusty brown-colored, naugahyde style living room set. It had end tables and two lamps. They told me they would buy it for us, and we could make payments to them. I cried and said yes, thank you. The store delivered it that afternoon. When we got back on our feet again, we paid them back in full.

One night Barney and I always joined hands and prayed before we went to bed. While we were praying, I began to see visions…I saw big military trucks and oriental men loading white women and children into those trucks, here, in our homeland. Barney began to prophecy to me. I was fasting for a few days. He said, "continue to fast because I am going to give you the Revelation of Jesus Christ." I really didn't know what that meant, but in later years, did I ever find out!

My aunt called me that week and said there's a revival at the Capital theatre; I went and took the children. I sat close to the door in case Kristi cried. That little preacher looked back at me and said, "lady in the lavender blouse…God has a word for you. Continue your fast and I will give you the Revelation of Jesus

Christ." Number 2... hearing it twice... meant witness; and there I had the witness. I thought it would happen right away, but it was 7 years before it began to happen. Before God moved on me, I didn't like to read the word; I would struggle and lay it aside. But when God moved, I couldn't leave my bible alone; now it's the love of my life.

Barney and I were going to church a lot now. Barney was beginning to preach here and there. He received the Holy Ghost on his knees, in a little country church, with the evidence of speaking in an unknown tongue. God really began to use him; Barney would lay his hands on someone, pray, and they would be healed. He also began to prophecy things to come. We fasted a lot. We bought a house in Red Bank, TN, a suburb of Chattanooga. We were so excited that Barney was working; he got a job at Sears and Roebuck, selling whole kitchens...the appliances and the cabinets. He would go to the customer's home and draw up the plans. Sometimes I would go along with him. Other times, I worked on redoing my kitchen cabinets, painted and wallpapered, and put down new tile. Barney put in new double sinks and a new countertop, and a new stove and refrigerator. I loved doing the redecorating.

I went to work at Paco Sportswear, sewing on their power machines. I did very well. They were able to reduce the price per dozen on the items I was sewing because I was doing so many and making way over production. God really blessed me. God also blessed Barney as he was the top salesman in the plumbing department at Sears.

We felt led to open a little mission in Chattanooga, on Main St., and started having services. God really moved and did a work there. People came and gave their hearts to God. There was also a lot of healing. We enjoyed that.

At one point, I got so very sick; I couldn't sit up very well and definitely couldn't stand up. Barney took me to the doctor, but I didn't get better. Barney was taking care of the kids and I was just lying in bed. I was praying... asking God why he wasn't answering our prayers for healing. I told the Lord I felt so alone. All of a sudden, a song came to me... God was giving me words. I asked Barney for paper and a pencil. I could hardly see to write; I was so dizzy. But I scribbled the words down. The name of it was, "I Am Never Alone". The chorus goes, "Oh beautiful song, my soul shall sing; my heart shall rejoice in thee. I'm never alone for I have the Savior; He's walking, ever walking, with me." After I wrote the song, I got well. Praise the Lord; **God was moving**.

My sister, Carolyn, found that she had to leave her husband. She got a divorce and came and lived with Barney and me for a while. She had had a little baby girl. We had a nice apartment in the basement where she moved into. She went to work where I worked, together. We took our babies to the babysitter together. It was nice. Then she met her new husband and started a new life.

My brother, Leon, lived with us for a while, too. He was just 17 or 18 and was lots of fun. He would come in from work and start rubbing his hands together and say, "let's go to the Huddildy House. It was the Huddle House down the road. Their menu included a T-bone steak, fries, Texas toast and a salad for $5.95. We loved it. And Leon and I would go to Warner Park and Lake Winnipesauke, ride the rides, and eat popcorn and cotton candy.

Barney and I were beginning to get back on our feet again. That year we went on a vacation to Miami, FL. Barney's sister, Sue, still lived there, so we visited her and enjoyed it very much. We went to see the Sea Aquarium and other little sights for the kids. One day we went over to visit Sue, had lunch, and were relaxing afterwards. Barney asked Sue if he could go back to a bedroom and rest for a few minutes. He had a strange expression on his face. Sue noticed it and asked me if something was wrong. I was used to seeing it, so I told her, "I think the Lord is speaking to him." She was amazed and asked me, "does this really happen?" I said, "yes, it does to Barney." After a bit, Barney came out and asked Sue if she would watch the kids for a few minutes. He said, "I need to talk to Pat." She said, yes, of course. We drove down the road and went to Howard Johnson's Restaurant and ordered a steak. Then Barney began to tell me what God told him in the bedroom. He said, **"your days of working for man is over!! From now on, you will work for Me. Go home, put your home on the market, sell your possessions, and evangelize for Me. You will travel for Me. I will show you 5 cities to start, and I will lead you to the place I want you to minister. Trust Me, I will meet your needs."**

It scared us. We were afraid of the unknown. Barney said his steak spoiled on his stomach; he was so "shook up" (his words). My heart was broken; I loved my home. I had put lots of time into my home. Be careful you do not put anything before God. You could lose it. God must be first in our lives.

The Lord told Barney He was calling him on a long fast before we did anything, so, Barney started on his fast. I was doing yard sales to get rid of everything. I just walked around and cried, looking at my little worldly possessions... not worth a lot, but I was grateful for everything. The Christmas before our vacation to Miami we bought yard toys for the children. We got them a large swing set with a slide, and little wagons and tricycles.

Barney's fasting made him so skinny and very weak. But it finally came to the day that his fasting was over. The kids and I were so happy to see him eat. I fed him cream of chicken soup and juice, and about 3 crackers. It went down well and stayed on his stomach. After 47 days, he was doing good.

That weekend, we took Barney's mother to the cemetery to put flowers on Pop's grave. Mom was a little chatter box. Barney and the kids and I were trailing along behind when, all of a sudden, Barney just fell down. Gregg started yelling, "daddy, daddy!" I made him be quiet; Mom hadn't seen anything…she was still walking and talking. We helped Barney up. If mom had seen that, she would have been upset. She, like lots of people, didn't understand that when God tells you to fast, it is not going to hurt you.

We sold a lot of things, but the swing set and the dining room set, and some of the toys, did not sell in time. I called a friend up in the country and gave those things to them. She was so happy; she had been praying for a table to eat from.

After we sold or gave away everything, we loaded the car with what we would need and hit the road for the Lord Jesus. We owed on the car, and we didn't have a church supporting us. It was us and Jesus. Right then, we took out our insurance policy with the *Sonship Company*… it never failed us, praise the Lord!

We went to Columbus, GA. We were going to rent a nice apartment but, all of a sudden, I got so upset and started to cry. I told Barney, "this isn't where we're supposed to be!" So, we kept on looking and saw a sign on the front lawn of a home that said, For Rent, 1 room. We stopped and rented it. We had to share the bathroom. That was so hard on us and the kids. But the man of the house got us in touch with the preacher there in town. He wanted a revival; we had a good meeting. They provided a large house for us to live in… and stocked the fridge with food. And I love rocking chairs… there was one in each bedroom, and in the living room, and on the front porch. ***Isn't God good!***

The church was across the state line, in Phoenix City, Alabama. We made the connection in Columbus, GA, and had the meetings in Alabama. We told everybody "bye-bye" and hit the road again.

We headed for Huntingdon, West Virginia. God tried our faith there. It was hard to find an apartment. Then we felt the Lord had led us to a church. We

Our first tent

The tent going up

Barny praying for People

Barney Preaching

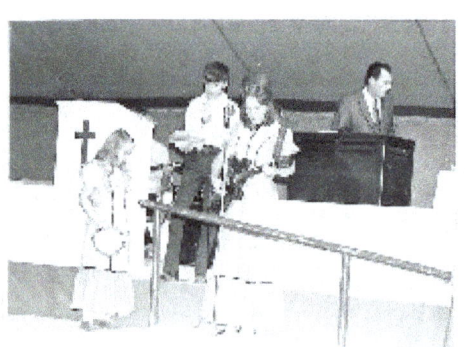

The Kid & I
Leading The singing

These are pictures of us in the meeting across the country serving the Lord

went on Wednesday evening to their service. The people were not very friendly. They didn't come shake our hands. I think one man did shake our hand. The preacher wouldn't even make eye contact. After the service, he left out the back way so we could not talk to him.

That night I had a dream that we were in the church and all the congregation and the preacher were speaking. The preacher was telling the people not to talk to "that man back there", pointing at Barney. He told them, "he is a warlock!" I had never heard that before. The next morning, I asked Barney, "what is a warlock?" He told me it is a male witch, and why was I asking. I told him, "why don't we just go on?" But Barney wanted to go back Sunday morning, and so we did. The people wouldn't have anything to do with us and the preacher shunned us. We left, drove around a lot, and asked the Lord, "where do we go now, Lord?" He sent us to Topeka, Kansas.

We drove around awhile, trying to get the mind of the Lord on where to go. We had driven down a dirt road and saw a man working on a fence. We stopped and asked him if there was a church close by. He said no, there was not, then asked how we came to be there. Barney told him. He invited us to come and sit on the front porch for iced tea. We did, and as we talked, he was moved… you could tell. He invited us to spend the night. His wife wouldn't come and sit on the porch with us. When he took us into the house, it was so awkward. He called his wife into the living room and told her we were staying overnight. The poor thing was so unfriendly. She and I fixed supper; after we ate, I cleaned the kitchen. When I went into the living room, she was combing her hair. It was auburn and hung all the way to the floor.

After we went to bed, I could hear her talking through the wall. I could tell she was upset. The next morning, there was not breakfast…just coffee. He said that we must leave. We thanked them and left. His wife was not happy, and I could understand maybe she didn't feel well. He should have talked it over with her.

We searched for an apartment but couldn't find one we could afford and that would take children. Finally, we saw a little white building that had a sign "For Rent". We stopped and Barney went in to inquire. The old gentleman said, "no…no children". Barney just stood there and looked at him when, all of a sudden, this man started to cry. Then he said, "I've got a roll away bed that I can put in the apartment for you." *God moved for us again.*

It was hot and boring there. I read stories in Reader's Digest, wrote letters, and tried to entertain the kids. I didn't want them outside very much. I tried to read the Bible, but I didn't understand it. I had forgotten that God told me in 1965 that He would give me the Revelation of Jesus Christ.

We went to a beautiful church, but they had just finished a revival. They were nice to us. The man playing the organ kept looking at us and, after the service, people were shaking hands. The organist came back to where the kids and I were waiting. He said, "Sister, if God were to bless you, would you need it?" I said yes, so he gave me an offering.

It came time to leave the little white house... the rent was up. We were just driving around, again, looking for something we could live in, or a church we could work in. We turned a corner and there were people just talking in the street. We realized that the one man was the organist from the church we had visited. He saw us and waved for us to stop. We did. We visited for a minute in the street and then he told us to pull in and we would have some iced tea. He inquired about what we were doing. We told him we had to vacate the current dwelling, with hardly any money for another rental. He said, "well, you can move in with us; we have room upstairs." I noticed he didn't consult his wife; that gave me reservations. But we didn't really have a choice, and so we accepted.

We went to the previous house to get our things, and when we came back to this man's home, there sat the pastor on the porch. *God was working* on our pride; we were so embarrassed. *God was moving for us*...helping us to overcome our pride and providing us a place to live. A couple days later the power steering went out of our car. The boys scouted around the junk yard and found a used part and they went to work installing it. When they finally got it done, they gave us a 3-day revival at their church.

I worked with the brother in the church office, making up the bulletins. It was a trial to live there. The man was so hard on his wife and children. Barney and I disapproved, and we were honest with him. We told him he whipped his children too hard. He said, "the bible says, the blueness of the wound drives out the inward wickedness."

He fried eggs for him and Barney, but his wife and I, and the kids, ate powdered eggs. The Lord had a learning experience for us during those three weeks. We appreciated their sharing their home, but we were glad to hit the road. I missed his wife; she was a sweet, humble woman. She was a nurse; he drew

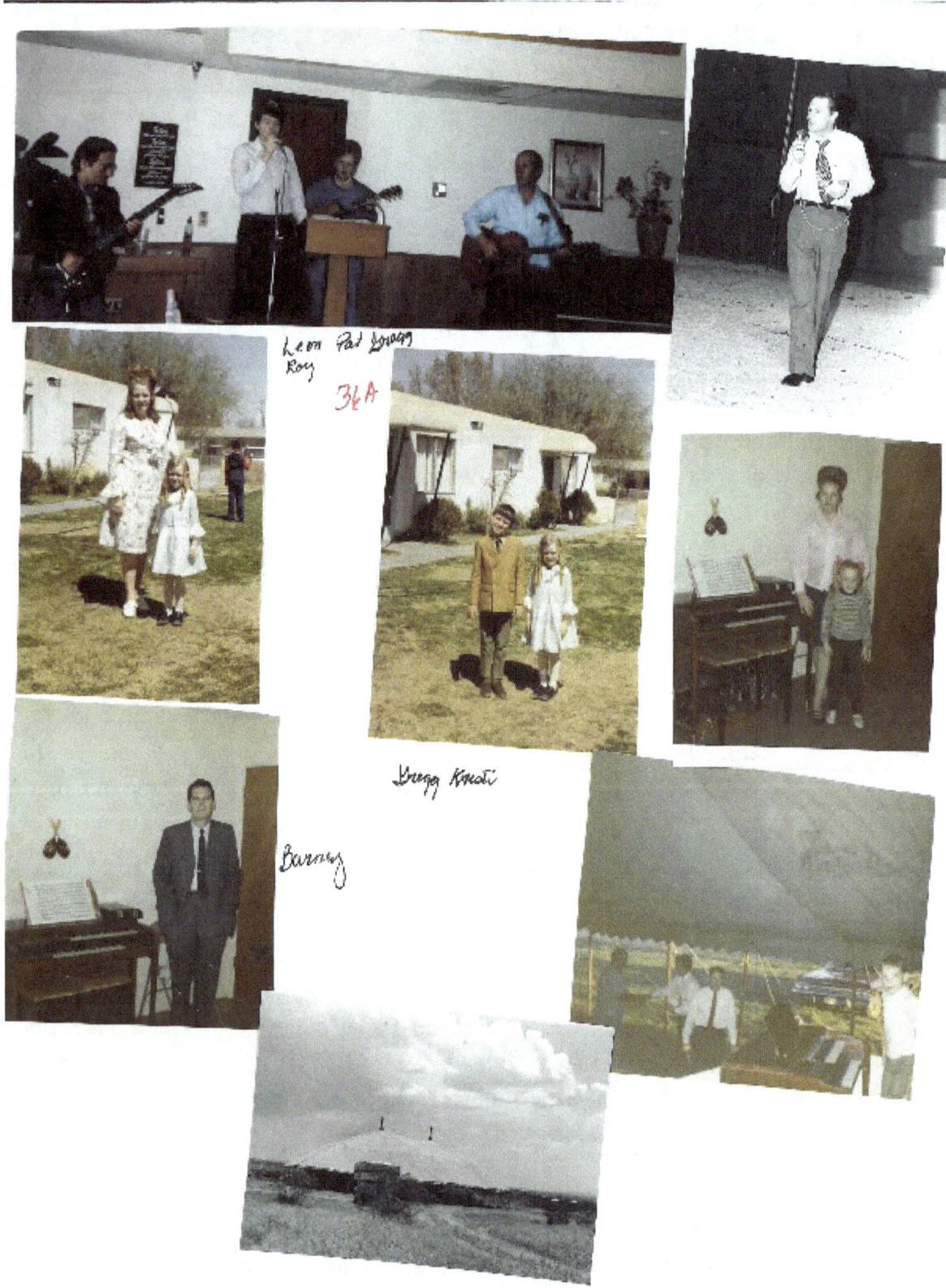

Leon   Pat Gragg
Roy

36A

Gragg Kristi

Barney

disability. I thanked his oldest son for letting us have his bedroom. He said, "I didn't have a choice." That made me feel so bad.

We went, then, to Kansas City, MO, and rented a hot, upstairs apartment with no air conditioner, and no fans. We paid one week's rent and had no more money. We went to a church on Wednesday night. They were having a revival. There were only 4 people there... the pastor and his wife, and the evangelist and his wife. But they had services like there was a full house. They also told us of a small church that might want a revival.

We had to wait a day or two until they had church. We needed to get out of the apartment. It was hot and not at all comfortable. When we moved in and I started cleaning, the table leg fell off, and I opened a cabinet and the door fell off. At the last meeting we attended, they gave us what they called a "pounding". It was food stuffs from government issue. We were thankful for it. I thought there was a chicken but, when I opened it, it was only the backs and necks. I cried! But they had given me some flour, so I decided to make dumplins. I opened the flour, and it was loaded with weevils. I put paper on the table and poured the flour out on it, picked out the weevils, and made the dumplins.

I had put the table out on the porch as it was cooler out there to eat. We lived upstairs but there were steps to the bottom floor. I took the bowl of dumplins, set them on the table, and went back in to get the iced tea. When I started back out the door, there was a little, half-naked boy with his hand in the dumplins, trying to get one. When he saw me, he ran down the stairs, I called to him to come back but his mother called him. His stomach was distended from hunger. I was so upset; I wanted to feed him. I sent Gregg and Kristi down to invite him up, but his mother refused. I went myself to ask and there was another little boy... a twin... in the same condition. The mother shut the door on us. I felt guilty; I had been crying, having a pity party. At least we had something to eat. I took my trash down and the cans were running over. I saw her can was full of wine bottles.

I started picking up trash around the bins. My little son, Gregg, had been wanting a Zorro whip, red and black. We couldn't afford it at that time. As I picked up a box, it had something stuck to the bottom of it. It swung downward and scared me. I thought it was a snake, but it was a red and black Zorro whip. I took it inside and washed it; then I got some shortening and oiled it really good. I laid it in the window for the oil to absorb. The next day I gave it to Gregg.

The landlord had come by and wanted the rent. Barney was fasting so he was in the bedroom. I was taking care of things. I told the rent man that we would pay it in the next couple of days. He threatened to throw us out if we didn't pay. I closed the door and cried again. Then I thought about the Zorro whip. *God was moving* for even the little things. So, "shut up Pat" and get on with trusting the Lord.

We went down to the little mission the evangelist told us about. We talked to the pastor; she said she would talk to the elder and let us know.

The next day, we went to the zoo; it was free. We looked at everything; the kids enjoyed it; we did a lot of walking. We didn't have money for lunch. Barney looked over at me and said, "I don't think there was ever a time I didn't have money for a Coke. A few minutes later that evangelist walked through the gate with his wife. He said, "Hello Brother Padgett. I didn't expect to see you here. Man, it is hot. You want a Coke?" Great! Did we ever want a Coke! He told his wife, "you and Sister Padgett get us all a Coke." ...and so, we did. See, *the Lord was moving again* in the little things.

We went back to the Mission and they wanted a revival service. In the meantime, we received an offering in the mail. We paid the rent. *God's moving... God really moved* in that meeting. The pastor was a woman. She called Barney up front and told him that God showed her he had heart valve blockage. She laid her hands on Barney and he fell out in the spirit. He felt something happening in his chest. *God moved again!* At one of the services, someone threw smoke bombs in the door, trying to stop our service. But we continued on.

There was a nice lady going to church there who wanted to show us some hospitality. She asked us to go home with her one day to have waffles for lunch. She couldn't find her waffle mix at first but finally found on top of one of her cabinets. That didn't bode well with me. She did make them, but they were so rancid, I could hardly eat them. Barney didn't eat waffles, but the kids loved them for the taste of the syrup. She also gave Kristi a beautiful doll.

When Barney was preaching, he related the Coke story. One of the brothers came over afterwards, handed Barney some money, and told him to buy a big Coke. It was a good meeting; plus, some street kids came and accepted Jesus then, too.

We got to move on when that meeting was over. We went home for a break. We had a meeting in Georgia with some folks. We were praying when I saw a large number 37 in a vision. I knew what it meant; the Lord had already told me he would call me on a long fast. I didn't say anything on the way home. We were staying with my mother for a few days. Barney spoke up and asked me, "it was a number, wasn't it?" I said yes. In a few days we headed for Baton Rouge, LA. We went to a church outside Baton Rouge and started a Revival. It went three weeks. Everybody loved it. We got new people coming in and accepting the Lord, being baptized with water and the Holy Ghost. A couple, that was coming to church, came by one day and brought bags of clothes for the kids. There were coats, shoes, socks, pants, shirts, dresses, and underwear. What a blessing. **God moved again.**

I was fasting, only drinking water, so I was getting pretty weak. God was taking care of me just like he did Barney. When the days got long, I needed something to do. Barney went by the college and picked up a typing instruction book for me. I taught myself to type and I loved it. The pastor's wife fed Barney and the kids every Sunday. It smelled so good. I stayed in the living room, looked at magazines, and let my mouth water.

Then the revival wound up and we went back to Chattanooga for a few days. I had about 3 or 4 days left on my fast. The day before the fast ended, I was weak, so I lay on the bed next to the kitchen. Mother was talking to me while she cooked. There was a lull in the conversation, and I began to sing, "Oh to be His hand, extending, reaching out to the oppressed; Let me, let me, touch Jesus so that others may know and be blessed." Suddenly, a mist came into the room, swirling around the ceiling like a cloud. I saw a masculine hand reach down through the mist, and a smaller hand reached and took something from the other hand. The power of God was so strong and sweet, my mother was shouting in the kitchen. The next day I got to eat... a half cup of soup, and a half cup of orange juice. Shortly afterwards, it came back up like a fountain. It scared Mother; she cried. Barney told her, "don't be upset; God will take care of you when you fast." And he did. I was fine. I ate the same again and was able to keep it on my stomach. And I started to regain my strength.

While we were in Chattanooga taking a break, Barney and I went down to a drive-in one evening to get something to drink. We pulled up and parked. In a few minutes, a nice big, yellow car pulled up beside us. We looked over and the man was looking at us. In a minute, he crawled out and came walking to our car. When Barney rolled the window down, this man spoke to Barney and said, "The Lord has a word for your wife. May I get into the back seat?" We said yes. I had been praying God would let me work in the background and not out front. I did not feel comfortable being out front.

This preacher began to speak to me. He said, "God has heard your prayer, but the work I have for you to do is with the people. You have a music and a singing ministry, you know that. But you will minister the word, also; God will give you Holy boldness and take no thought, I will give you words to say. But you have to be out front.

God told Barney, in the beginning, He would give us five cities to start with. Barney received 4 cities and we were waiting for the fifth one. One day God showed me the city, Springfield, MO. So, we got ready, told everybody good-bye, and headed for Springfield. We arrived in the city; it was a pretty place. We found a nice apartment easily enough. We found the people in the church to be nice country folk. They had a woman pastor, Sister Norma. Her brother played music for her...piano, organ, and guitar. He was talented. Her Daddy came and sat on the platform like a big, old bulldog. He tried to run everything. He called Barney a jackleg preacher, but his daughter was struggling to obey God. Not him so much.

We had a long revival there. Sis Norma was so nice. She took us to her home for Sunday dinner; it was very good. While we were there in revival, the pastor of another church in town came to visit the service, along with a few members of his church. After the service, he came and greeted us. He welcomed us to town and, also, to visit his church. He presented us with some of his booklets, and an offering. His name was Bill Britton, a very nice man. He later came to our apartment and interpreted some of the visions I had. We had dinner with them while we were in the meeting.

Mother came to visit us from Chattanooga. She wasn't with us very long when she wanted to go home, and we didn't have the money or time to get her there. She cried and fussed until we told her husband to help her get home. I think he was mad at her for coming and he wouldn't send her money.

We met a lovely country family, Sis Tommie Parker. I really loved her. She would cook us the best meals and we'd stay the night. They were like family. Her daughter and I took the kids to the circus, and we walked all the way. The "youngins" loved it.

One night at service, God and the Holy Spirit came over me and I moved out of my seat and went to the back of the church, with my eyes closed and my hand in the air. I didn't know where I was or where I was going. But I placed my hands on a lady in the back row, and she passed a tumor from her body. Barney prayed for people all the time, and those things happened for him. But I didn't do that very often. Brother Britton invited us to stay there with them to help in their ministry and to learn as we went. Barney didn't feel that was what God wanted for us, so we moved on.

We went back to Chattanooga for a few days and were invited to hold a revival in Falling Water, Tennessee. We started that revival and it went really well. People were happy for it and, at the end, the church gave us a large truck and a small Army tent to hold meetings. We were going to set it up in Calhoun, Georgia, but God said, "no, take your truck and tent and go to Albuquerque, NM, and leave Wednesday of next week. It was Friday when God gave us these instructions. Barney had $30 to is name, but we said, "Ok Lord." We started preparing to go and, by Wednesday, we had $130. The night before we left, Barney had a dream. He saw a spark plug blow out the engine of the big truck. He told me about it and wondered if it was really the Lord showing him it would happen? Well, outside of Fort Smith, ARK, it happened. We were stuck on the side of the road until they could run down the road for a spark plug. Once that was fixed, we were on our way again.

When we arrived in Albuquerque, I said, "This God-forsaken place?" It was so barren, no grass, no trees, or vines like in Tennessee. I thought maybe God won't make us stay very long. Fifty-one years later we are still here. God gave us a love for the southwest.

We lived in Albuquerque for 2 years and, in that span of time, we lived in a small, two-room apartment in the South Valley. You couldn't drink the water; it had gas in it. There was no place to park the truck. A nice neighbor down the road let us park the truck at his house.

We started to check out the churches in the area. We went to a Spanish Pentacostal church; Frank Guterriez was the pastor. They wanted us to hold a revival the next week and we were looking forward to it. In the meantime, we had $3. I went to the store to get what groceries I could. I found a loaf of bread for 25 cents. As I walked around trying to find bargains, I kept having the urge to buy a box of crayons and a coloring book. I knew I couldn't, we needed groceries. But it wouldn't stop hounding me, and I kept finding myself at the rack with the crayons and coloring books. When I finally checked out, I had a coloring book and crayons, and I worried all the way home about what Barney would say. He was smiling when I walked in. I was so nervous, so I just spilled the beans and told him what I did. I said, "I don't know why I did it!" Barney said, "I do. The kids were in the other room praying that you would bring the book and crayolas." He said, "I heard Kristi tell Gregg, 'don't pray anymore; I've got it in my hand.'" My little ole youngins were smiling from ear to ear.

We set up our tent on Isleta Blvd., across from Blake's Lotaburger, who provided the lot free of charge. It was getting cool at night, so we kept the tent curtains down with some big coal oil heater going. The Indians came from the reservation and wrapped up in their blankets. We had good crowds despite the cooler nights. There was a preacher from a church down the road, who came every night, with others, and sat in their car to hear me sing. They thought I was from Nashville. We got acquainted later and had a revival in their church. We got close to those people.

We also met a sweet minister and his wife who had a huge, beautiful tent set up on Coors Rd. He came to visit us and, also, invited us to come up to see them. He was going to give Barney some stakes for our tent; he was concerned it might come down. We were visiting and having coffee in their trailer when a huge dust devil hit their tent and tore it down. They had a beautiful Hammond organ with big Leslie speakers. A quarter pole hit the organ and split it in half. I had been wanting a Hammond organ; I cried and cried; such a waste, I thought. Except, God always has a reason for what he allows to happen. We may not understand it, but just know that God is in control.

When we got back to our little tent, it was standing tall; we were relieved. But, just a few days later, it blew down. The Lord told Barney to repair it and put it back up. I sat in the middle of the tent, sewing it up, working all day. It was quite a job. The sun was hot, and the canvas was hot, but we put it up and had more services.

A little red-headed preacher we met came in one night with a ham. Barney called him his "little, red-headed Raven." **God moves…** It finally got too cold, so we had to take down the tent and pack it up. At some point, we went to Springdale, Ark. We took the tent and set it up. We had a meeting. All the motels were full, so we lived in a pup tent. That wasn't easy. My kids were fascinated by the crawdads coming up out of the holes in the ground. Soon there came a storm, the tent fell on our heads, scared the kids, irritated Barney, and aggravated me. Then the Lord let us know that we had to give our tent and truck, the chairs and platform, to a preacher that has visited us from Oklahoma City. We didn't want to do that. We took off to Springfield, MO, to visit our friend Tommie Parker. We loved visiting with her. She fixed a big meal. We went to bed. About 2 am., Barney woke me up and said, "we have to go back to Springdale and give that tent to the preacher. I went to the kitchen and made coffee for the road. Sis Parker came in and found out what was up. She made a big breakfast and said, "you cannot leave without eating." *God moved again…*

Throughout our ministerial days, God always moved for us. It really came close sometimes and, I hate to say this, but this is the way we would feel sometimes. We were desolate: no money, not much to eat, and 3 voices were talking to us. There was: the voice of our need; the voice of our greed; and the voice of our seed. The voice of our need was a worry; the voice of our greed was depending on the natural man and not God; and the voice of our seed was saying, "obey God and rely on God; know that if you obey, God will meet your needs. The seed that God has planted in you defies world condition." God's heart is moved by my need; God's hand is moved by my seed. That means God takes action.

We started the meeting in Brother Guterriez's church, "The El Sendera LaCrux". They sang all the songs in Spanish; I played in Spanish, I guess. They sang in the key of "F". Barney preached ministerial healing and comfort and spoke words of prophecy, telling things to come. It was a wonderful revival. Brother Frank had us move into a little pink house he had, that had been empty for a while. We cleaned with joy and happily moved in. It was larger and fairly nice. Gregg started school in the first grade. I hated to see him go. The little fellow's trials started; some boys tied him to the fence on the way to school. A larger boy came along and untied him. Gregg was devastated.

From there, we moved to Viola Road, where the kids would go to Barcelonia school. The teacher was hard on Gregg, shoving his head into the desk and pushing her nails into his head. I had to go take care of that situation. My friend, Mary Ann Blankenship's daughter was receiving the same treatment. But mercifully, it stopped.

The apartments on Viola Road were nice but when we drove over, they wouldn't rent to Barney. We needed a first and last month's rent, and a deposit. But we only had one's weeks rent amount. Barney came back to the car and said, "Hon, why don't you go in and try; maybe she'll rent to you." I was nervous but I went in and went through the same spiel to rent. She just kept looking at me. I promised her that when the rent was due the next week, we would have it all. She said, "okay, I'll let you have it for a week and, when the rent is due, you pay all." I went back to the car with a spirit of elation. Barney said, "how did you do it?" I told him I promised her all the money next week. He asked, "how are you going to do that?" I said, "God won't let me down." We had no furniture. There was a refrigerator and a stove. A sister we had met in a revival gave us a bed. A lady we met in another church where we had revival gave us a couch and chair.

When I went to church on Wednesday night of the next week, I sat down in the pew. A hand came over my shoulder and dropped an envelope in my lap. I said "thank you" over my shoulder but didn't even know who it was. When I got home, Barney was in the bed. I went into the bedroom, turned on the light, and began to throw "twenties" on the bed. Barney was shocked. It was exactly enough to pay what I promised the landlord.

We lived in Albuquerque for two years, but the Lord started to lead us away from that city. Eventually, God led us to Reserve, NM. We rented a house with two smaller houses on the back lot. We could tell the people of the town were wary of us; some of them were downright rude. We rented a small building and started a church. By then, several members of our family were there, and three families from Albuquerque also followed us to Reserve.

We had some lean times after we moved to Reserve. My sister, Carol's husband, left her so she got food stamps. We would go to Silver City to shop. I would have $15 on me for shopping. I wanted to buy more groceries. Carolyn said, "you can get food stamps with your low income." I asked Barney... he didn't want me to get them. I kept on him until he gave in and I prepared to go on Friday to get the food stamps. The night before, I had a dream that two catholic priests came to my door in long black robes to give me food stamps. I knew that meant I should not do it. I was wide awake, and I saw a mist form up around my ceiling and, in it, were two large bags of flour... and then Jesus's face appeared in the bags. He spoke to me, saying, "Have not I provided for thee?" I broke down. I felt so guilty after all the times God has provided for us.

Since the Lord had spoken in prophecy in 1965 that He would give me the Revelation of Jesus Christ, I was so excited when I received the overwhelming desire to read and study God's word. I began to understand truths I had never seen before. We had a constant flow of people in and out of the house, and that made it difficult for me to study. I asked the Lord to wake me in the early morning hours for study. I was awakened at 2 am and began to study every morning until the children would wake up for school. Kristi told me, not long ago, that she would wake up and feel comforted because I was by her bedroom reading God's word; I didn't know that.

We bought a cow, some pigs, and made big garden, and sewed a patch of Pinto beans. I canned 700 jars one year of: vegetables, meat, pickles, apples, pears, pear preserved, jellies, sausage, and stew. We loved it! One bad part during this time was that I lost the diamond out of my wedding ring while canning turnip greens. That hurt me so much to lose that.

We had some fun out of my city-boy husband. The cow we bought was to come in "fresh" in March. Barney said, "won't it be nice to have fresh milk?" I said, "yes, and a baby calf." Barney said, "what?! You mean we are getting a calf, too?" We had to laugh. When we started to plant potatoes, Barney grabbed a bucket, filled it full of whole potatoes, and started off. We said, "where are you going?" "To plant my potatoes" he said. We told him that he didn't cut them. He said, "what do you mean, cut them?" Again, we had to laugh. One day he wanted to make some lye soap. He read about how to in a Mother Earth News. He proceeded to make it and put it out to set. Sometime later, he came to the house, crestfallen. He said his soap all leaked out. Guess what? We had to laugh. Barney was a good sport about it though. He would laugh, too.

When my family came, they lived in the two small houses on our lot. Some more people came and rented a couple houses up the main drag. It wasn't long until my sister, Carol, her husband, Lewis, Brother Tommy, his wife, Martha, Brother Leon, his wife Jeannie, Bother Bobby, Sister Sue, and even my mother, stepdad, two younger sisters, Alice, and Nancy and her husband, and Bill Nix... all showed up. The Lord provided us a new tent and another truck, and a better car to work for the Lord. We were going in meetings all over... Las Cruces, Alamogordo, Albuquerque, Artesia, Roswell, Hobbs, Las Vegas, Farmington, Silver City, Deming, Lordsburg, Espanola, Taos, Gallup, Raton, Clovis, Tucumcari, Sante Fe, Belen, and Socorro. In addition, also a couple towns in Texas, some of the towns a couple or three times.

The Lord had spoken to us that he would give us some land to go out from, but also to come back to a place of our own. We started driving around, looking for land for sale. We couldn't seem to find what would meet our needs. We were praying that God would lead us. I had a prayer room out behind the house. I would go out every day and pray and read. Barney asked me to pray God would show me where we would have land...so, I did pray. This is what the Lord showed me: *It is a wood of the oak woods, to the southwest, 8 miles from Jerusalem.* Neither Barney nor I understood what it meant so, we went on with life, working for Christ.

Barney went to Gallup to set up a meeting. The real estate guy got in touch and said he had property to look at. We found out it was in Datil and met him to look at it. We had a good feeling about it and found we liked it. We made the arrangements to buy it and made a good deal. And there we were, just like the Lord promised. We had a place to come back to.

We came every week to work on the land. We built fences, dug ditches, cut trees, and trimmed them out for fence posts, plowed and fenced in a garden area, dug water lines, dug sewers, built a church on the hill, got a well dug, and got electricity put in...and got our mobile home moved in.

Let me back up a little... The day everyone came up to choose where they wanted to put their mobile home or travel trailer, they all decided. Barney and I were last; Barney wanted to be centrally located. The part that was left had a huge ditch running through it. I saw this ugly little tree in what would have been my front yard. I asked what it was, and someone said it was a scrub oak. *Praise the Lord!* I remembered what God showed me when I asked Him about land "in prayer." There it was... the wood of the oak woods. The Lord knew I was used to the great might oaks. "To the southwest" ...we were in the southwest part of the state, the country. We bought 4 40-acre plots, and we're in the southwest 40, in the southwest corner of that forty. What about "8 miles from Jerusalem? Eight is the number of regeneration and Jesus Christ. Jerusalem...the spiritual place where Jesus lives in his vessels of clay. So, if we had any doubt about where we are, there is doubt no longer. *God moved again...*

It certainly was a lot of hard work, developing that piece of land. We didn't have heavy equipment; we did it all by hand, devising ways to make it work. And, in the meantime, we were going all over the state, and Texas, evangelizing. God was blessing us. He blessed our "going out" and our "coming in". In the meantime, God was showing Barney things that would happen in the future, and he would give it as a word of prophecy. I was receiving a spiritual understanding of the word.

We built a church on the hill behind our house. We built it from scratch. We furnished it and began to have service. We had some wonderful services. Everyone got settled in their own dwelling places. The boys got jobs, some at the sawmill in Pie Town. Our kids started school in Datil elementary. There were 7 kids going to school from our group.

In some of the towns, people thought we were a cult. They were afraid to let their children associate with our children. It made it difficult but eventually the people began to know us. Some of them even came to church with us. I started having bible studies in some of their homes. I started singing and playing my guitar and that opened the door for bible study. I got invited to sing at weddings, churches, funerals, graduations, and anniversaries. I began to get to know lots of people. The rest of our group had become acquainted in town; they were working at different little jobs.

My sister Nancy was married to a nice man named Bill. Bill had epilepsy and he passed away. We had his funeral and buried him on our property. It was a traumatic time. Later, his sister came to take his body back to Tennessee, to be buried in their family plot. The other twin of Nancy, Alice, had married our tent man's son while we were living in Reserve, NM. Then all the girls came up pregnant...my sisters Carol, Alice, and Nancy, and my brother Leon's wife Jeanie.

My mother and stepdad came out and lived here a while. My mother didn't care for New Mexico; she called it Mexico. So, they went back to Tennessee. Then my sister Carol and her family moved to Alabama. Tommy and his wife, Martha, Bobby, my brother, Alice and Johnny, and Nancy had already left. Leon and Jeanie were the last to leave.

Leon had built a nice house and had a business. He asked me one day if I would like to have a craft shop. I said, YES! So, he and my brother-in-law built a little shop for me in the corner of his building. He had a garage in one side. I had a grand opening; I named it The Country Sonrise Shop. I started making lots of wood crafts. I made potato bins, bread boxes, paper towel racks, rocking horses, rocking chairs, stepstools, corner shelves, trash bins, and different kinds of shelves. I did some paintings and sold them. I made dolls and called them "Pat-a-Cake dolls". I made welcome signs, lots of wall hangings, spice cabinets, bachelor chairs, afghans, and Appalachian door harps... just some of the things I made.

We were still going in meetings, ministering the word all over the state, and in Lubbock, TX, and Odessa, TX. We also made a garden. Barney and Leon built a large greenhouse. We felt so blessed. Later, Leon traded his place for a business in Socorro, so I had to move out of my cute little shop.

Gregg worked in the forest, pulling logs out with the big horse we had. Kristi graduated from Quemado High School. They both left for college the same year. I sure had a hard time with the "empty nest" situation. Kristi went to Las Cruces;

Gregg went to the "School of Mines" in Socorro. Kristi later quit college and got a job. College wasn't her cup of tea. Gregg went 5 years and got a physics degree. He went to work for Aero Jet Ord. In the meantime, I had moved into a building on Highway 60, in the middle of town. Barney and I created a pretty craft and gift shop. We carpeted and built walls. I was there for six months when the owners sold it. Marvin and Tudi owned the building. I had a dream one night that Tudi Ake and I were together crying. I knew I would have to move. About a week later, she drove up and came in. She was very nervous; she was lighting up a cigarette. Her hand was shaking. I asked her, "how long have I got?" She said, "we'll give you a month." So, I was on the move again. Then I was home awhile swinging yard work, working on the greenhouse, making custom drapes for my bedroom. Barney and I installed a carpet. We built one room at a time; sometimes it took a while because money was tight. Sometimes Barney got tired and would quit for a while. When he built the back bedroom and bath, he did the foundation, then stopped. I waited and he wouldn't get back to it. I named it the "venture to procrastination". Then he built the wall and stopped again for six months. I named it the "venture to futility". But one day he said, "I am gonna finish that room!" He did and I loved it, such a pretty room. He tiled the bathroom with ceramic tile that our friend, Jake Snyder, gave him.

We went in a meeting to spread the gospel. We were having a meeting in the northern part of New Mexico. It was a little cold, but this young man wanted to be baptized, so we broke the ice, and Leon and Barney went out in the water and took Matthew. OH! He was cold when he came up. I wrapped him in Barney's wool robe. He asked Barney, "are you going to tarry with me?" Barney said, "no, you're going to tarry with the Lord. We had to laugh; he was a neat and funny guy. We were so glad to have a place to come home to. **God is so good...**

We went in a meeting in Hobbs, NM; we had the tent, and it was hot. We met some folks that love the ministry. They eventually followed us to Reserve, then to Datil. While we were in Hobbs, a man came in a pickup, parked right behind the tent, close, and threatened to drive his truck through the tent. He was behind the platform where all our instruments and sound system was located. I was on the platform, playing the organ. Barney told him to leave, or we would call the police. He left but he came back the next night and tried to do the same thing. Leon went to talk to him, and he got a little rough with him, but when he saw inside the truck cab, he saw the man's legs were withered. Then Barney went to him and tried to talk to him about getting his life right with God...but he left. The next night, he came back with a big bag full of steaks. He had tears and said he was sorry. He came every night and listened.

An old black gentleman would come and get excited in the Lord. He'd say, "Lawd, toughen my ole hide but don't toughen my heart. Soften my heart Lawd."

We also had a meeting in Hobbs, NM. Sis Hazel was a lady pastor; we had a good meeting, but we were glad to leave Hobbs both times. We also went to Raton twice…once in the tent, once in an auditorium. We went to Clovis twice… once in the tent, once in an auditorium. When we were in the tent, it was so hot. The wind blew all the time, but God really made it worth the sacrifice. One night, shortly after we went to bed, these boys came with a truck and a car, and drove as fast as they could around the trailer… and then around the tent. We were so afraid they would hit the stakes. We had to hurry and roll in all the windows; sand was coming in all over.

One year, we were in Espanola, NM. It was a cold winter, and we were in the travel trailer. Our heat went off and Barney had to get up and try to get it back on. He had his robe on; the wind was blowing, the robe was blowing out on each side, and Barney's hair was sticking up. He was totally aggravated. Leon and Jeanie's trailer was close enough for them to be able to see and they were watching Barney and laughing. Leon did come out to help, though. Barney came in and I said, "what's wrong hon?" He said the "thang" won't light. I said, "oh, no!" He said, back to me, "gripe, gripe, gripe!" I put my head under the cover and didn't say another word. I was just concerned for him out in the cold. We laughed about it later.

When we first got to Espanola, we ran into Leon right outside of town. He was pulling the Terry trailer and had slid off the road. He was down between the highways; Jeanie and I went on in but not before I gave Leon a thermos of hot coffee. When we got to the motel, the snow was getting deep, and I almost slid into our travel trailer. Barney got a tow service to go get Leon.

We had a good crowd of people who came out, even in the bad weather. They were hungry for the word; many were healed of different illnesses. We learned our lesson, though… no more travel trailers in the winter. From then on, we stayed in motels.

After we got settled here in Datil, we planted an orchard. We had peach trees, apple trees, pear trees, an almond tree, cherry trees, and a grape vine. Sad to say, we found out what ground gophers were. They began to chew the roots of our trees. They just started to fall over, and when we picked them up, there were no roots, just sticks. The grape vine died. Needless to say, a few hundred dollars down the drain. I tried every way to kill the gophers. I even dug way down in their tunnel, hooked a hose to my brother, Leon's, truck exhaust and ran it down in its tunnel? Suddenly, a funny-looking creature came out of the hole. It scared me so bad that I jumped straight up out of the hole, yelling. I found out it was an oversized water dog. One day Leon drove up and I was in the hole; he said, "what's the matter Pat...you can't beat 'em, so you're gonna join 'em?" I tried poison bombs in their holes, and water, and propane from the gas tank off the travel trailer... then live traps. But they won!

Our tent blew down in Espanola, in Albuquerque, and almost in Clovis. We fought all day to keep it up. Over the years of our tent meetings, we had some real interesting times. We went to Roswell and set up the tent. I got bronchitis; the kids got chicken pox. We were in a motel apartment. It was so hot, Gregg got diarrhea, along with the chicken pox; both kids were in bed. I fixed sandwiches and water for Barney and the tent man. I had to get the kids in the car and run the lunches over. When I got there, the men were sitting under the tent with hand-dog faces. I knew something was wrong. I asked...they said the electrical inspector red-tagged the pole for the tent. I felt the spirit of God move on me and I told them, "I don't accept this; *God will move!*"

Gregg got so bad with his diarrhea, I had to put paper towels in his underwear. His bowels were running like water. The next day, I took the kids (Gregg lay in the back seat) to deliver the lunch to the men folk. They were torn up; someone had stolen all the tools. Barney went to see about our electricity, and our tent man took a nap. They didn't have the tools to put the platform together. So, I took my little, sick youngins' and searched for yard sales. We didn't have much money, but we got enough tools to complete the job. I had to try to find a tree so the kids would be in the shade while I searched for the tools. We all survived and started the night services.

We had an altar... a bench in front of the platform with a large piece of carpet for people to kneel on. A woman started coming to the service. She tried to go on the platform and lay hands on Barney. He rebuked her and told her to sit down. Sometime during the day, she came and cut a piece of the carpet. We found out, she practiced witchcraft. I guess she thought she would take the piece of carpet and put a spell on us. She came back that night and started up on the platform; she laid her hands on our tent man. Barney went to her and rebuked the devil. She let out a cry! …and ran into the street and never came back.

We saw a lot of people come to the Lord there in that meeting. I guess that's why we had such a hard time; "Ole Slew foot (the devil) was mad!" We met some friends there who helped us in the meeting. Typically, we came home, rested up, did laundry, cleaned house, and got ready to go again. We went to Artesia… set up and had a wonderful meeting with lots of good people who pitched in and helped. A little lady came in one night and sat on the front row. She said, "I've come to see you." Barney looked at her for a minute and he said, "God's going to heal you tonight." She said, "I know." After Barney preached, he prayed for the sick. He prayed for the little lady; she was dressed to the nine's, with a big flower on her breast. Come to find out, she had a restaurant there that she and her husband operated daily. She said she couldn't make change because her hands were so full of arthritis. Her husband had to rub them down every night to get enough relief to be able to sleep. Barney was able to help her.

She knew all the doctors at the hospital, and she told them God had healed her. She could make change, and she was able to sleep well, so the doctors came every night, sat in their Lincolns and Cadillacs, and listened and watched.

It was such a hot job, but we had to waterproof our tent. After it was done, we would return home for a while. We met friends there that we kept in touch with for years. Before we got our new tent, we went into lots of the towns and cities and rented meeting rooms in the motels, club houses, school auditoriums, or recreation centers. During the school session, we had to leave the children with someone; my sister kept them most of the time. It was hard for the kids, and I felt like I was missing out on so much of their lives. I would sit in the motel and cry, but I would go to the Goodwill store or the thrift shops and hunt for toys for the kids, to try to make up for my absence.   I found them some really nice things. I tried to keep a happy face for the kids, so they didn't resent our leaving so much. Obeying God was so important. We all had a sacrifice to make… even my little children. My kids were good kids. They thought more about what we were doing for the Lord than what they wanted.

Barney felt led to go to Alamogordo again. We went, and we had a good meeting. We got to see some old friends again. There was one couple who had a shoe store; they took us over and gave us new shoes. What a treat!

One day, some young boy came on the platform and took the bass guitar that Gregg played, and the amplifiers. But we got them back. *God moved once again.*

We had our travel trailers set behind the tent. At one time, a big bull snake wanted to move in. We turned him around to go the other way, but he would turn right back around. We finally put some water in a garbage can lid. He crawled over and drank the water. I had never seen a snake drink before. The he went on his merry way.

Every evening, when the service started and we began to sing, all the cows in the pasture across the road would hang their heads over the fence and listen. But, when the preaching started, they would wander away. Does that sound familiar?

When we packed up to go home, it took a couple days or more. I hauled the organ, musical instruments, and the sound system in a Ford truck. We had no air, no radio. We would leave the hot desert and climb up the mountain to cool air. Kristi and I would hang out the windows and let the cool air hit us in the face.

Next, Barney felt we should go to Odessa, TX. We packed up and went. It was a good meeting; lots of word going forth and healing taking place. We met a nice family who also worked for the Lord. The kids played music and sang with their mom and dad. Gregg got a crush on the pretty little girl.

Some people came and supported us. The lady bought us shoes, and they brought us food. After the meeting closed out, we went on to Lubbock, TX. That meeting wasn't as good, not a good turnout. We were tired and glad to get home. Once we got home, we would have to catch up on everything. Sometimes we would have an orchard and a garden, also a greenhouse. Some of those people working with us would take care of things while we were gone. I know it wasn't easy for my sister, Carol. Their house was small, and the kids were crowded.

The episode of Queenie: We had a dog that was our tent dog and would go in the meetings with us. But she was also our family pet. One day, when we were living in Reserve, Queenie was hit by the Catholic priest while she was crossing the road. He just kept going. She was spinning around in the street, trying to get up. We got her inside and prayed for her. She was nursing a litter of pups, so we had to take them away while she was healing. We were so worried about her; we didn't know if she would walk again. One night, in a dream, I saw her running with a slight limp. And that is how it really happened. She always had that slight limp afterwards. Later, after we moved to Datil, she was running with our male German Shepard, went across the highway and started chasing sheep. The owner shot the male and killed him. But the shot for Queenie was high and laid open the flesh on her back, right down to the backbone. She came home and climbed on the steps. I knew she wanted prayer, so we prayed for her and the wound closed, and she healed up fine. We were so thankful. Another day, she came up missing and we began to worry. My brother-in-law found her with her head stuck in a log. The ants had bitten her jaws and she was swollen so badly that she couldn't get out of the log. He brought her home, and again, we prayed. **God moved** and saved our little dog.

While life is moving on, these kids of ours are growing up. Kristi and Gregg were ready for high school. Kristi wanted a haircut with bangs and pierced ears. Gregg played chess by mail and wanted to be a millionaire. He went one year to Quemado high school, and then he stopped. We bought lessons from American School. He studied every day and made good grades, graduated, and got accepted at the School of Mines in Socorro. Kristi stayed in high school and graduated from Quemado high; later she went on to state in Las Cruces. The only way her dad would let her go to the prom was for me to go with her. I was so embarrassed, and I guess she was, too. Kristi quit college and got a job. She said she wasn't college material. It disappointed us but we wanted her to be happy.

When we weren't in a meeting, I would go to the church and fall on my knees and cry out to the Lord on behalf of our situation. We didn't have any finances coming in, and we didn't have any other means of support, unless Barney picked up an odd job or hauled firewood for someone. But God always moved for us; we never went hungry. One year Barney cut and hauled 30 chords of wood. Barney was self-taught. He learned to build, garden, haul wood, cut the trees. Of course, our life was dedicated to working for our Lord and Savior, Jesus Christ. But we had to occupy till He comes. He tells us in Ephesians 6:10, "when we've done all we can, to stand; to stand, therefore." He also said, "seek ye first the kingdom of God and his righteousness, and all these things will be added to you." God's word cannot fail.

My brother, Leon, bought a large building and one day asked me if I would like him to build me a craft shop in one side of it. Of course, I said yes. He and my brother-in-law built it; it was so nice. I had a grand opening. The community really supported me and the shop. I bought saws and wood tools, and I started making country wood items.

We were still going in meeting at least once a month. We had a church in Datil, and we held services there twice a week. A lot of the family was with us.

We were striving to be a witness to the community because, when we first came, they thought we were a cult or devil worshippers.

The Lord brought a wonderful woman, and friend, into my life. Her name was Thelma. She was my New Mexico mother, and the Lord knew I needed her. She always introduced me as her "daughter". We went everywhere together. We made cookies and candies together at Christmas, took walks together, went out to lunch, and went to church together. She was a good Christian woman and I loved her.

I had some good friends, Mary and Vernon, and one day they showed up at my door to tell me Thelma had been killed in Taos, NM… in a head-on collision by a drunk driver. I wept and grieved; I missed her so much. One day in November, I was at the back of my craft shop and sanding some wood. Suddenly, there was a large Monarch butterfly, fluttering in my face. I felt Thelma's spirit. She used to tease me, and I felt that teasing spirit as the butterfly fluttered close to me. When Thelma had come to visit me, she had a certain place she always parked. That beautiful butterfly flew over to that spot where Thelma parked and then disappeared from my view. I said, "Thelma, is that you teasing me?" I knew the Lord used it as a sign to let me know Thelma was happy. Thelma helped me to become acclimated to the village of Datil. She introduced me to everyone. After I lost Thelma, Sue, a friend of Thelma and me, began to come in and pray with me. We would call each other and read our Daily Bread together. One time, Sue began to feel the spirit while we talked on the phone. She said, "I'm coming in." When she got to the shop, we rejoiced together. It was so comforting. When I would sing at church, she would always cry. She was more spiritual than people realized. One night I got a phone call from a friend telling me Sue had also been killed by a drunk driver on Sedella Hill. Her husband, Pastor Jake Snyder, was following behind her and saw her lights go off the road. When he got to her, he knew she was gone. It was so devastating to him and their grown children.

I had a good friend, Nancy, who I felt was like a sister to me. She was good to me; she promoted my singing and music and, also, my handiwork at the shop. She would bring me food at lunch time and tell me I needed to eat. She was always in a hurry. She always attended the Cowbell meetings and the Extension Club meetings. I was glad she was there. We used to have an exercise class, too. We would do different exercises and dance fast. One day Nancy said, "let's dance the Larospa" (not sure of the spelling). We started to dance, and I got to laughing so hard that I was about to wet myself. I was trying to tell her that and pull away, but she kept holding on. I could not hold it, and there appeared to be a running puddle. Nancy was shocked, but we laughed about that for a very long time. One night I had a dream that we were at an extension meeting. I was looking for Nancy; she hadn't shown, up and I was concerned. Then I saw her come in. She was beautiful in a pink, shirt-waist dress. It was shimmering. I went to her and said, "well, I am glad you are here." She was looking right through me; no one else seemed to see her there. A few days later, she passed away.

For a while, we had some livestock… horses, cows, pigs, goats, and chickens. One day, the goats went to town. Someone called and we had to go bring them home. All our cows were named: Daisy Belle, Donna Belle, Nellie Belle, Tinker Belle, and Oscar Belle. Some of the chickens had names, too. We had a rooster, mean as a striped snake, named Dapper Dan. He was a pretty thing, but one day he went after Kristi, chased her down the hill. She threw the water down and was screaming. I was mad; I took off after him. He ran back up the hill to the pen. I went in, got him by the feet, and ducked him in the water and held him about three times. He stayed in his place after that.

One of our cows, Tinker Belle, was such a pet. She would come when we called, just like a dog would. She would put her two front hooves up on the steps. She wanted to come up on the porch.

We had a big Palomino horse, named Pam. Before Gregg went to college, he worked for the Hanson sawmill. He pulled logs out of the woods with Pam. She was a big horse! He made enough money to buy himself a truck. Then he went to college. After he got a small car, easy on the gas, he gave the truck to his dad. Before Gregg worked in the woods, he got sick. All the symptoms seemed to indicate he had Rheumatic fever. His joints were inflamed, and his fever was so high. He would not go to the doctor. He just wanted us to pray for him. We prayed constantly. God healed him after many days. We were so thankful.

Later, Gregg had to get a physical… either for college or for a job, I do not remember. Barney and I went with him. Barney went to do some shopping while I waited for Gregg in the doctor's office. I was reading Ladies' Home Journal, "Can this marriage be saved?" I remember because God performed a miracle that day. Suddenly, I became aware of activity. The two doctors were running back and forth, and I wondered, what's happening? The doctor came out and told me they wanted to send Gregg to a heart specialist. It scared me for a moment. The doctor said, "he won't go; you've got to talk to him, Mom." Then he went back to Gregg.

Then, at that moment, I saw a gold light coming toward me, and it seemed to go in my heart. I felt God's power; I knew he was telling me "no, Gregg is healed." So, we left. Gregg said, "we've always depended on the Lord to heal us, and that's what I'm doing now." Later, Gregg had a physical and got a clean bill of health. His heart was well and strong. Once again, **God moves**...

The Lord called Barney on a 21-day fast. He took the camper over in the woods and camped out. The kids and I would take him water and visit with him. We had different family members that would come and go, from here in Datil or Reserve, to Chattanooga, TN, or Mississippi, Georgia, or Alabama. But you know, if you are going to serve God, you have to be steadfast and immovable.

One day we got a big surprise... Kristi was pregnant. We were really concerned about the situation. But, when Josh was born, we fell in love, and it stayed that way. They lived with us for two years. I was working at the shop five and six days a week. Kristi helped here at the house with her day. It was such a joy to come home, tired, and see Josh and have a good, hot meal. I did all kinds of wood crafts, which were time consuming.

At one point, Kristi told us she wanted to move to Albuquerque and get a job. We hated to give them up, but she needed to be on her own. She did well; she got a cute apartment. It still broke our hearts to leave them. Barney and I went as often as we could to see them. When we had to leave, I would cry, Kristi would cry, and Josh would reach out his little hand and cry "mamaw." That was so hard. Kristi eventually went to work at a day care so she could keep Josh with her.

In the meantime, Barney and I were lonely. I had a couple friends who sang with me. We enjoyed that. We went a few places and sang at churches, and I loved that, too. We made a CD and named it "Jesus, Write my Song." I just trust people were blessed as they listened to our gospel CD. The Lord had given me the words to "Jesus, Write my Song." One day I asked Leon to sing a certain song for me, and he could not remember the words, so he said, "I can't remember it Pat, I'm a blank page." I heard the words in my mind, so later I wrote the song. I didn't know at the time that Leon was in the first stages of Alzheimer's disease that slowly progressed. He got to where he had a hard time doing his job. He was the electrical contractor. He has worked so many homes in Datil, but slowly he couldn't do it anymore. He didn't have money at first, and he wasn't old enough to draw social security. We had him move into the trailer that was on the property here. He lived here for several years but, finally, his kids had to put him in a home. We miss him so badly. I have been able to go see him several times. He is in Colorado Springs, in an Alzheimer's facility.

Kristi met a man, Patrick, and they got married. They have always lived in Albuquerque. They eventually had a little girl; she was a doll. They had their little family going. They bought a trailer and lived there several years. Then Kristi found a nice house she loved, and they bought it. The kids both graduated from high school. We had dedicated both children to God when they were born. Our faith has been tested with those grandchildren. But we claim the scripture, raise a child up in the way they should go, and when they are old, they will not depart from it. Jesus never fails.

We used to have Bible Study around the community at different homes. We enjoyed it. I would sing at them, and teach some, too. I sang at weddings, funeral, parties, anniversaries, graduations, and church services. I also had my craft shop going. I made everything I sold, so it kept me plenty busy. I got lots of orders. People would come in and ask me to pray with them about some problem in their life, or they would tell me their problems… or they would call me on the phone with prayer requests. I would come home to get Barney to help me pray.

Nancy Wellborn named my shop, "The Soul Station"; I thought that was neat. Barney went over and preached at their church the Presbyterian, one time. And Nancy came to our church and fellowshipped with us as well.

One day I was in my garden, sticking beans. I had picked an arm load of sticks and felt the prick. I dropped the sticks and a black widow fell off my arm. She was so black and shiny. I began to feel something happening in my body. It was an uncomfortable feeling. I ran to the house and told Barney. He laid his hands on me and prayed for me. He said, "you'll be alright." I laid on the bed a few minutes and I began to feel better. I got up and went back to sticking my beans. **God moved again.**

Barney had the old truck in the woods, picking up dead wood and limbs. The truck started rolling down hill, and Barney ran and jumped in to stop it. He didn't get his leg inside the truck. It got caught between the truck door and a pine tree. It tore the pant leg off and scraped his leg very badly; it was a bloody mess. He crawled into the house and asked me to pray. I laid hands on him and prayed. I was so upset, I wanted to hover. He said, "go on now, I'll be alright." I went back to the garden and worked. About an hour later, I saw him walking around, and then

Kristi's
Wedding Day.

The day my son presented
to me this beautiful
Guitar.

My Shop in Datil where
I made many types of craft
items.

Barry Alyssa

Josh

Josh

Josh

Kristi Patrick wampa

Alyssa
59B

59
¢

the truck started, too, so I knew God had touched him. *God moved again*... God never let us down.

We had a greenhouse and raised some vegetables in it. The gophers underground ate the roots of our fruit trees in the orchard. We only had peaches one year. As I said before, I fought those gophers with smoke bombs, poison, gas, truck exhaust, and water, but they won! My nephew could get them with metal traps. We had ground squirrels, tree squirrels, chipmunks, rabbits, racoons, skunks, deer, and elk. They eat the tree leaves, scrape off the bark, eat the flowers. They are beautiful, a novelty, but also a nuisance!

Our son, Gregg, is living in Branson, MO now. He is a wonderful musician; he plays guitar, lead, and bass guitar. Before Gregg moved to Branson, while he worked at Aero Jet Ordinance, he took us on several vacations. We got to go places and do things we had never done before. We had so much fun. When he had to go for training in Portland, Oregon, he sent us a couple tickets and we flew there. He rented a pretty, red car and we traveled up the coast; at every place that looked interesting, we would stop. One time we went to the Grand Canyon and the Petrified Forest; another time we went to Utah, saw Zion Park and other parks, and we went to some Indian ruins... I cannot remember the name. He also took me to the Precious Moments Chapel; it was a beautiful place, I loved it.

After Gregg moved to Branson, we would go to see him twice a year. It was such fun. We saw every show there, I guess, and went to a lot of fun places. Gregg was so good to us. He went out and bought us both a comfortable chair to sit on. He waited on us; you could not have asked for a better host. We always had good food. He made cream cheese pies all the time. Barney always loved that. He loved the trips just like I did. We would listen to Gregg's CD, easy listening music, and we would watch the countryside go by. It was so beautiful. There were trees, vines, flowers, and grass everywhere...dogwood blooming... Red Buds blooming in the Spring. We always went in October and in April. He took us on the Branson Bell, a cruise ship, and the Branson train, down to Arkansas, to see a show about the Shepherd of the Hills.

Gregg has made many CD's, and he has worked in some shows in Branson. Barney and I have had some wonderful vacations with Gregg, and our trips to Branson is always such a pleasure. Nobody could be better to us.

Barney's "jail ministry" is going strong. He has had a jail ministry in Socorro for 16 years. He sure does have a burden for those boys, and they love Barney.

Until the rules changed, he would take them ey glasses, bibles, Christian literature, rosaries, and ink pens. They would make little gifts for us in return.

Sometimes, we would be in town at a restaurant or Walmart, or a gas station, and here would come a young man running up and saying, "Hey Barney." Sometimes they would hug him and tell him how well they were doing, or that they got a good job, or are buying a house, or attending bible study. One young man said that Barney saved his life. It was so encouraging to see those boys get off the drugs or liquor and start serving the Lord.

We slowed down going out in Evangelistic meeting as we had less money and were getting a little older. We started to have service in our home and had quite a few people coming. God was really moving and changing our lives by His word.

Then, we went from our home to the Montosa campground as friends of ours had bought the property. We had service under the open air pavilion until it got too cold. For those times, we moved into the camp kitchen. We had service and potluck every Sunday. God sure did move by changing our lives, giving us wonderful healing and freedom from bondage. Then God moved on our friend to build a church. One day we were having service and God moved on me to prophecy to our friend that "he would build a church for the Lord" and he did...a very beautiful church. That is where we are having service now. God has never failed; He has always provided a place of worship.

My husband was our pastor. Until Leon got too sick, he helped us, and we always worked together. I missed him so much when he had to leave.

One day, a few years later, my precious husband fell and hurt himself very badly. We took him to the hospital. He stayed for a few days, then came home and kept getting worse. We got him ready to go back to the hospital. My son and I were carrying him to the car, and he died in our arms. I didn't realize it at the time. I thought he passed out, and I was talking to him. It broke our hearts, and it left a large hole in my life. Barney is the only love for me. Through the good times and the bad times, we were always together.

When Barney went to be with Jesus, my community gathered around me and supported me. There is nothing like your brothers and sisters in the Lord. You know you've got a family. My heart has cried out for my husband, but the Lord Jesus has been my comfort. My church sent me to Branson to be with Gregg for a while. After some time, the Lord sent me a young man to help me with everything around the place... my water, the well, the tank... He took care of things for 2 years. We could talk about the Lord; he is a Christian young man. When he had to go to college, I requested prayer at church for the Lord to send me a trust-worthy person. The next Sunday, the man followed me out to the car and said, "I heard your request last Sunday and I would like to be that man. I just started praising the Lord. Now this man helps me all the time. I can really depend on him and his wife; they are so good to me.

You know, we never realize how much our partner does until they are gone. And what a comfort they are just having them by your side. I see Barney everywhere I look.

The Lord has been so good to me since I lost Barney. He truly lets me know I am not alone. My church put in a wall gas heater for me to supplements the pellet stove. My pellet stove started acting up so they got me a large propane heater. It is wonderful.

My oven quit on my cookstove and a couple families bought me a new stove. My windshield was busted on my car and my friend that helps me, and his wife, said they wanted to wash my car. When they brought it back, I had a new windshield, a full tank of gas, and an oil change. I just went to their house crying to thank them. I was so thankful; *God moved once again.*

I have been going one day a week to practice singing with the girls I made the CD with, about 10 years ago. I park my car at a friend's house and one of the girls picks me up for the rest of the trip. One of my headlamps was out, and the film on the other headlamp was so dim. One day, I picked my car up to go home, but these friends invited me in for supper. When I started home, they walked me to my car. When I started the car, the lights seemed so bright. I got out and looked; I had two brand new headlights. *The Lord moved again.* The two of them were grinning and being very sneaky.

One couple in the church took me under their wings from the very beginning. Another couple helps me a lot. I told everyone, "I have stock in the Sonship Company. *"God never fails."*

Barney was the Pastor of the Chapel of Living Water at Montosa. When he passed away, they asked me if I could take over and teach as well as sing and pray. I said yes. So, I sing and play at the Datil Cowboy Church, then go to Montosa for church. I do Bible study on Monday evening at Melynda and Russell Walraven's. I love them; they feel like my kids. They are a blessing.

Every other Sunday, I have Bible study with Kristi and Patrick. My Monday night Bible study has gone through Revelations twice. Now I really know what God meant when He said, "I'm going to give you the Revelation of Jesus Christ." I saw a vision while I was living in Reserve. I saw the earth hanging out in space. There was a huge Bible that covered the earth. Then I saw Jesus emerging from the Bible, letting me know that Jesus's word is coming to life in us. In the midst of our worldly chaos, God is moving where sin abounds. Grace does much more abound.

After I lost Barney...or should I say, Barney went to be with Jesus...Kristi and Patrick sure have come to my rescue. Patrick takes care of my repairs around the house. He keeps the rat population down; they buy good poison. Kristi helps clean; they pull my flowers out in Spring for me; Patrick waters and gets my cooler going in the summer and winterizes it in the Winter. Kristi buys groceries for me along with yarn, cards, and gift bags, etc., for my crafts. I can always talk to Kristi about problems. She buys me blouses and sweaters all the time. I am running out of space to hang them.

Kristi and Patrick had her dad's picture hung in a restaurant in Albuquerque. This restaurant has a Veterans wall; Kristi had a small photo restored and enlarged to be put on the wall with the others. What a surprise when we walked in and I saw my handsome husband's picture on the wall. I cried. She made me a beautiful picture book. Kristi and Patrick also took my brother, Leon's, leather cowboy boots and had a purse made for me, from them. What a surprise on Christmas day...to open that box and see the beautiful purse. It was so thoughtful and sweet of them... also, to remember Leon when I carry it.

This year 2020 has been so chaotic with the Covid-19. We didn't get to have a lot of our activities. Our craft show is one of the things the community looks forward to. We have been doing it since 1981. It's always so much fun, and it brings in a little revenue for the community and scholarships for our high school seniors. Our ladies get together and enjoy one another's company.

One wonderful thing happened in 2020. God blessed us with a beautiful granddaughter, great granddaughter, and daughter, ...Alora Trijillo; such a joy. This Christmas, we dedicated Alora to the Lord. I know she is not ours, but the Lord's. He loaned her to us for a while. All the kids participated, laying their hands on her and praying. I loved that. We had scripture and a poem. Alyssa was going to sing, but she was hoarse and couldn't.

Throughout the years that I have lived in Datil, I trust I have been a Christian example. I have sung at many funerals for people I've loved, but it's hard to do. I always tried to do it with love. Some of the older gentlemen would ask ahead of time if I would sing for them. I hope I have lots more time to work for Jesus before the Lord calls me home. The fields are white onto harvest, and my children need more loving and teaching.

THE LOVE OF GOD

Written by Gregg Padgett

(For his mother, Pat Padgett)

The Love of God needed a vessel, those years ago, and found one in that little girl of reddish-blondish hair and innocent blue eyes. But that special vessel came to know adversity, early on, as Satan tried to thwart God's purposes. And, despite years of abuse in many forms, and much toil in the fields of cotton, along with rearing of the younger ones, the seeds of God's Love were growing in this special one.

As she grew into adulthood, the innocent girl would meet the man to whom she has been faithfully married for over a half century. But this was a marriage that God built, since He had great purpose in the ministries that would be a perfect accompaniment to each other. God anointed her singing and playing of string and organ, so that He could speak directly to the heart through His chosen vessel. As she was faithful in this, God also gifted her with the writing of song, as He continued to write the song of her life in Him. Farther along, God then planted His own word seed in her heart so that He could truly reveal Himself to her, as shown by her many visions. This resulted in Biblical teaching of power and authority, to reveal the mystery of the living God. And this vessel of God continues to heed the call today, in the dispensation of these gifts and talents, despite adversity to the point of death and opposition that comes in many forms. But, does the Love of God stop there? No, it is just beginning to manifest itself fully in the many facets of a willing and obedient vessel as we shall see.

Throughout her life, she has been a dutiful wife and mother, even though she endured great sacrifice early on to obey the call of God upon her husband to obey the fulltime ministry. This involved being uprooted from their home site and traveling to many different and strange places. But, despite the loss of home and income, she stayed true to God and her family. But, in the effort to obey God in ministry, many times this bereaved mother had to leave her children behind in the hands of others. And that doesn't mention many other adversities, such as: the hot big tops, cramped living quarters, frequent traveling, communal living with others, and constant visits from church members. Verily, the demands of obedience and sacrifice are great upon the life of true ministry.

But this child of God has born and reared two handsome children, that were brought up in the holy fear of God. To be sure, there were many challenges as the children grew into adolescence, but this diligent mother stood steadfast in the Love of God throughout this difficult time. And, as they have gotten older, the children have not departed from their raising as God promised in His word.

Now, once the children had left home and the group members of the church had departed, this chosen vessel had to fill the void and find other channels to show God's love, by reaching out to the surrounding community. How was this accomplished? By starting a business of craft creations and selling cosmetics; by participating and singing in local churches and camp meetings; by joining local organizations; and by conducting community Bible studies. Barriers have had to be broken, but the love of God will not be denied... just like the little flower that finds a way to break through the asphalt.

So, how has the love of God been shown by this chosen one? By faithfully sharing the many talents that God has bestowed upon her. The love of God was on display when she sang at all the funerals, weddings, graduations, Christmas carolings, church services, and other special events.

This love has shined through all the customized craft items made from yarn, wood, and paint that have been distributed throughout the community.

And, finally, she has shared this Godly love by counseling and praying with those in need, as well as showing God's plan for mankind in community Bible teaching.

So, to sum up, let's look at the many ways the love of God has been manifested in the life of this virtuous woman. God's love has been shown through the many talents that this wonderful lady has been blessed with. And one of the first talents that she manifested was her ability to be a resourceful and industrious homemaker, having just that special touch to make a house a home, no matter what the conditions were. This hard-working vessel is accustomed to creating things from scratch... whether it be the cooking of a country meal, the crafting of a useful wood item, the crocheting or knitting of a yarn design, the penning of a new song, the sewing of a clothes pattern, the painting of a lovely picture, or the planting of a new garden...she does all of this with great skill and beauty, and many of these creations were turned into gifts for others, as the generosity of this beloved woman knows no bounds. Her gift giving is of mystical proportions as she could rightly be donned, "the bearer of many gifts." Oh, if only the blind eyes and deaf ears could be opened to see and hear the love of God that has been manifested in this dedicated vessel throughout her lifetime. She has only done the bidding of God that came naturally by yielding to the love of Christ, that must be shared continuously. Wow! What a blessing and leader this woman has been to her family, her church, and her community. Oh, what a blessed one!

The Dawning of a New Day

Written by Pat Padgett

For daughter Kristi's High School Graduation

Verse 1

Here we are, the day has come,

A new beginning, a victory won.

Some times were good, some of them bad,

And even though I'm happy, still I'm a little sad.

All of my friends are here today,

And very soon we'll be going our own way.

The happy times we have shared, doing things we shouldn't dare.

So many things we've learned; a greater knowledge earned.

Chorus

And there's the dawning of a new day, for each and every one of us.

The challenge for tomorrow we meet with hope and trust.

So here's to the memories of the class of '83;

A great tomorrow I can see;

But I won't forget my yesterdays.

The Dawning of a New Day

Verse 2

The time has come; we've made our plans.

We'll meet the challenge of every man.

To make a better world

For every boy and girl

The class of '83 will help to make it free.

Verse 3

It's time to say goodby. Oh my! How time flies.

I'll miss each one of you, my friends and teachers, too.

Thanks to all of those who gave

To prepare me for this day.

Thank you, Mom, for all your prayers.

Thank you, Dad, for just being there.

Raised by the Hand of Jesus

By Bobby Watts

Verse 1

The old van we were riding in came to a halt

At a bus stop in Western Tennessee.

The silence was so numbing to my four-year-old ears

As I waited for my Mama to be free.

There were tears in Daddy's eyes and in mine as I cried.

I watched Mama board the bus and ride away.

Verse 2

As they faded out of view Daddy slowly drove away,

Down that lonesome road we traveled silently.

Though I did not understand why, still my pain was so real,

And I wondered, why do these things have to be.

Even then there was a plan for those precious, nail-scarred hands.

Jesus reached down and placed a hedge around my life.

Chorus

It don't matter where I'm going, it don't matter where I've been;

Though the world may turn against me and I'll falter now and then.

There's no fear that I can't conquer; there's no battle I can't win.

I was raised by the hand of Jesus, and my heart belongs to Him.

Verse 3

Through the cotton fields of Arkansas and Mississippi we would go.

Daddy had to make a living his own way.

We labored in the fields by day, at night we'd work at home.

But I could still find time to close my eyes and pray,

To my father up in heaven, who gave me strength to carry on,

And I could always feel his hand upon my life.

Verse 4

Soon the years crept upon us and things began to change.

And the bottle soon became Dad's greatest friend.

The family scattered far and wide; it seems our love would fade,

And I wondered if our hearts would ever mend.

Through it all, there was Jesus; He was always by my side,

And I could always feel His hand upon my life.

Chorus 2

It don't matter where you're going; it don't matter where you've been.

Though the world my turn against you and you'll falter now and then.

There's no fear that you can't conquer; there's no battle you can't win.

You'll be raised by the hand of Jesus, and your heart belongs to Him.

The Children of God

A song written by the brothers and sisters of the Watts family.

Bobby wrote the chorus.

Verse 1A... by sister Carol Guess

We were taught many things when we were very small.

But how to trust Jesus was the greatest of them all.

Verse 1B... by Pat Padgett

When my mind was in bondage, and there seemed to be no way out,

God took the key of mercy and unlocked the chains of doubt.

Chorus... by brother Bobby

The same father, the same mother, we're all sisters and brothers.

We're the children of God, singing praise to the King.

We've known sorrow, we've known trouble

...but we don't live in that old rubble.

With a happy heart we're singing praise to the King.

Verse 2A... by sister Alice Owens

If we let Jesus' words dwell deep in our mind,

We will see his love flow like the river of time.

Verse 2B... by sister Sheila Smith

While much of my life I felt alone, without a friend.

But Jesus was there to comfort, He gave me peace within.

Verse 3A... by Sister Sue Smith

Through Jesus our Lord, whose work is already done,

We are given a vision of better things to come.

Verse 3B... by Leon Watts

By faith in God alone, I walked this way,

Through the long night of childhood into a brand new day.

Verse 4A... by Bobby for Billy

For too many years, the bottle let me down,

Till Jesus came and turned my life around.

Verse 4B... by Pat Padgett for Nancy

Through the eyes of a child, sorrow never seemed to end,

From the shadows of pain stepped a savior; He is Jesus my friend.

Verse 5A... by Bobby Watts

I know what it's like to walk on the battle field.

The scars and bruises take so long to heal.

Verse 5B... by Bobby for Tommy Watts

But it's worth it all just to know I'm in His will.

And through it all, I found Jesus; I found Him to be real.

Ode to Mom

by Gregg Padgett

MOM,

You're an inspiration to all, as you have heeded God's call,

To be a Tree of Life in God's Garden; sharing God's gift is a life of pardon.

Your sheltering branches welcome all who come,

To taste the fruits of goodness, enjoyed by some,

That nourish, soothe, and heal those with broken hearts,

Who, with your gentle urges, can make a brand, new start.

Your sturdy trunk has weathered the hurts and woes of life,

To support your fruitful branches that inspire you,

As sister, friend, mother, and wife.

Even when the rains of blessings do not shower down,

Your roots dig deeper as you strive for Jesus' power.

So, your tree stands stronger in a desert place,

Providing that oasis of love as you keep pace.

In planting your seeds of love, joy and peace,

That other souls might sprout forth without cease.

Till at last your life, that began as a seedling in the wilderness,

Multiplies into a forest of trees that sing forth praises of harmony and fullness.

God bless you, Mom

My Husband, The Gift You Gave Me
...by Pat Padgett

The man that stood beside me was my love and my life,

And I was so very happy to be his wife.

We started our lives together, and to each other we'd be true,

Doing what we wanted, Lord, we didn't think of you.

But You had other plans, Lord, for what this man would do.

You loaned him to me, but he belonged to you.

One day he heard You speak to him in a voice so soft and low,

And he answered back to you, Lord, and said, "Yes, I will go."

He lived his life for You, Lord; he kept his faith in God.

In love, he taught the precious word, as down life's road he trod.

To those who really needed You, he spoke a word that heals.

And because he obeyed you, Lord, the word is sounding still.

Now I see him walk away from me and leave me standing here.

I'm sad and oh so lonely, yet I will not fear.

Because I know where you are, hon, even though I shed a tear.

You're walking in that glory place you preached of all these years.